THE GIFT OF SEEING
ANGELS
AND DEMONS

A Handbook for
Discerners of Spirits

Susan Merritt, Ph.D.

PTLB
PRINCIPLES
TO LIVE BY
LIFE IS RELATIONSHIPS

The Gift of Seeing Angels and Demons:
A Handbook for Discerners of Spirits

Copyright © 2016, 2024 by Susan Merritt, Ph.D. Second Edition.
All rights reserved. Published by PTLB Publishing, P. O. Box 214, Roseville, CA
95661. (PTLB.com)

Copy Editing & Produced by:
Jennifer Edwards | jedwardsediting.net

Cover Design, Interior Book Design & Typography by:
Linné Garrett | 829 DESIGN | 829DESIGN.com

Cover Image:
Woodcut by Albrecht Dürer, Saint Michael Fighting the Dragon,
The Apocalypse Series (1498)

Unless otherwise noted, all Scripture quotations are from *The Authorized
King James Version of the Bible* (AKJV) and are reproduced by permission of
Cambridge University Press, the Crown's patentee in the UK.

Scripture quotations marked KJV are from *The King James Study Bible*. ©1988
by Liberty University. Center-column references and notes are ©1988 by Thomas
Nelson, Inc.

Scripture quotations marked ESV are from *The Holy Bible, English Standard
Version*. ESV® Text Edition: 2016. Copyright © 2001 by Crossway Bibles,
a publishing ministry of Good News Publishers.

ISBN 978-0990964186, Softcover

ISBN 978-997777802, Kindle (Published by SLM Publications)

Christian Living/Spiritual Warfare

Library of Congress Control Number: 2024915558

PRINTED IN THE UNITED STATES OF AMERICA

Dedicated to my parents,
who taught me to love
the Word of God.

Contents

Foreword

Yes, there are some people who see angels and demons. God has given them a gift to perceive the spiritual realm and what is happening there. At first, when Christians begin to perceive angels and demons, what they "see" may overwhelm them. God has signed them up for an adventure that many of them did not necessarily want. He wants them to grow in their faith to help others and the church win against the schemes of Satan. This book was written to help discerners of spirits grow in their faith and service to the Lord. I think you'll find it wonderful and mind-bending all at the same time.

All Christians embrace the idea that there are two halves to our current world: the visible (people, things, and other living creatures) and the invisible (God, angels, and demons). The Scriptures show us these two worlds in numerous passages: Exodus 34:5–7; Joshua 5:13–15; 2 Kings 6:17; Daniel 3, 5:5–6, 6:22, 8:15–17; 1 Kings 22:10–23; Luke 22:31; Acts 8:18–23. These passages tell us that different people have been able to see into the spiritual realm. In the New Testament, this ability is listed as a spiritual gift that God the Holy Spirit gives to certain people. The gift of discernment of spirits is the ability to see or perceive the actions of the spirit world. It is a gift from God that is not earned or deserved.

I have been privileged throughout my career as a pastor to have God send a number of people with these gifts to help in the ministry that I was engaged in. I refer to them as radar detectors. They can see what is invisible to the rest of us and can let us know what is going on in the invisible realms and whether an action or difficulty has its basis in an evil spirit or not. They are absolutely invaluable for a prayer ministry and for working with people who are oppressed by evil spirits.

As I have traveled the world ministering and speaking for Christ, I have occasionally mentioned this spiritual gift. I have talked about the fact that God has given some believers the ability to see or perceive the spirit realm. I usually have one or two people come up and talk to me privately about what happens to them. They often don't know what to do with all that they perceive. I let them know that if this is a true gift from the Lord Jesus Christ then it is a wonderful thing and they will be very helpful in prayer and ministry. On a number of occasions, people with this gift have warned me about situations and/or prayed for me and what they perceived was crucial to God's ultimate victory. I do not have this gift but have greatly benefitted from those whom God has given an authentic gift of discernment of spirits.

Susan Merritt was one of the people who stepped forward when I mentioned the wonders of this gift. She is a powerful prayer warrior and a gift from God to the church at large. When I began to give her a biblical basis about what was happening to her, she was thrilled and gave herself to prayer at an even deeper level. Because she has a scholar's mind, as well as this gift of discernment of spirits, I suggested that she do more research on this gift and write a book about how God wants to use this gift in His church. Dr. Merritt threw herself into the project and went on to receive a Ph.D. for her research and work in this area. I am very pleased to recommend her book on this spiritual gift. I believe it will help many whom God has equipped with this gift but do not know what to do and how to employ what they perceive for the glory of God.

This book is not for everyone, but it is for those who are called to a deeper level of spiritual warfare and for those who "see" the spirit realm and want to really help move the Kingdom of Christ forward. Dr. Merritt has really done her homework in this book and has interviewed a number of people who also have this spiritual gift. I am encouraged that she would take on this project and help us understand what has been in the Scriptures all along.

I do need to give a warning about this gift. There are people who have a counterfeit form of this gift that comes from the devil. This counterfeit form is getting quite a bit of attention in the movies, books, and television these days. This book is not about that type of false gift (i.e., the realm of mediums, séances, and the like). The Scriptures condemn all forms of divination. But what the Holy Spirit gives can be a great benefit to the body of Christ.

How can a person tell if they have the true gift and not a demonically inspired false gift? Dr. Merritt will cover some of this in her book, but let me give some basics. A person needs to have received this "ability" after they became a Christian, not before, and not as some kind of inherited ability from ancestors. This gift needs to move a person toward holiness. I have worked with people who have been so freaked out by what they began seeing when the gift started working in their life that they were almost paralyzed in their Christian life. They saw the church, the people, and even the pastor being attacked by evil spirits. The gift needs to line up with Scripture versus wild speculations and fanciful ideas. The gift should move a person to prayer and cause a person to study the Scriptures more. It is the Scriptures that bring truth, not fanciful dreams and images.

Kudos to Dr. Merritt for writing this book and to you for reading it. May you grow in the grace and the knowledge of the Lord Jesus Christ and use your gift well.

In His Service,
Dr. Gil Stieglitz

Introduction

Do you feel extreme distress and repulsion in the presence of certain people or in certain places? Have you ever found yourself sickened by an unexplainable stench nearby? After many years, I realized that incidents like these have a pattern in my life and that they are related to the gift of the Holy Spirit called discerning of spirits. When I first recognized this gift in myself, I began to search for information about it. Although I found plenty of books written on the subjects of gifts of the Holy Spirit, spiritual warfare, and demonology, there appeared to be nothing written specifically about this side of discerning of spirits.

"Discerning of spirits" is included in the list of gifts given to believers by the Holy Spirit as described in 1 Corinthians 12:7–11. Until recently, it has been rare for Christians to understand "discerning of spirits" as more than just being able to recognize false teachers and prophets, as found in 1 Peter 2:1 and 1 John 4:1–3. All Christians are admonished to exercise discernment to identify the lack of the Holy Spirit in the message of a given preacher or teacher in order to stop the incursion of heresy into the Church. This is a function of mature

Christianity, a result of reading, meditating, memorizing, and personally applying Scripture in a way that gives each believer vital insight into the truth or falsehood of what is supposed to be from God.

However, some Christians are gifted to be able to recognize the presence of angels, demons, and spiritual warfare, as evidenced by Scripture and sometimes by bizarre and inexplicable events. In searching for answers to my own questions about this overlooked and little-understood aspect of the spiritual gift of discerning of spirits, I found nothing written specifically on the subject of this gift being used as a weapon of spiritual warfare to protect the Church. But protection, prayer, and advanced warning of spiritual attack are precisely what the discerner of spirits is called to do.

This aspect of discerning of spirits is the subject of this book. It is written primarily to encourage and inform others who are confused about the isolating and sometimes perplexing manifestations of this gift. It is also written to enlighten pastors and other church leaders who need to know how to use the important information and warnings given them by the discerners of spirits within their churches. In this book, you will find information on what discerning of spirits is about, how to identify the gift in yourself, and what to do with it. The authentication of the gift is in the God-given, God-directed, and God-glorifying nature of the outcomes of the gift, as well as the implicit inclusion of the gift in the scriptural record. Unless otherwise noted, all Bible quotations are from *The Authorized King James Version*.

We live in an era of increasing wickedness, rampant apostasy, and barbarous persecution in the world. God is meeting the need for more people on the frontlines of spiritual warfare with an increase in both the number of people gifted in discerning of spirits and in the amount of information available that did not exist in previous generations.

Much spiritual warfare has accompanied the writing and revision of this book and so I thank every one of the prayer warriors who has covered me with protecting prayer, encouragement, and editorial help during this process. Thank you, too, to my husband, whose loving support and reassurance, even in the midst of my undivided attention to writing, has been essential.

CHAPTER ONE

The Gift of Discerning of Spirits

Acts 2 recounts the events of the day of Pentecost when the Holy Spirit was poured out on those gathered together. Jesus Christ had risen from the dead, was seen alive by many, and was observed ascending to heaven. Peter explained to the skeptics on the sidelines that all of the recent events, including the advent of the Holy Spirit, were foretold in Scripture. In Acts 2:38–39, he answered their subsequent questions with,

> Repent, and be baptized every one of you in the name of Jesus Christ for the remission of sins, and ye shall receive the gift of the Holy Ghost. For the promise is unto you, and to your children, and to all that are afar off, even as many as the Lord our God shall call.

The Biblical Gifts of the Holy Spirit

The apostles continued to demonstrate the gifts of prophecy, signs, and wonders. But notice that the gift of the Holy Spirit, along with the ability to do what God calls us to do, is not exclusively given to the apostles.

When we first accept Jesus Christ as our Lord and Savior, the Holy Spirit instills in each of us spiritual gifts that enable us to serve Him and accomplish His work and His will while we remain on earth. Merrill Unger, author of Unger's Bible Dictionary and books on a variety of biblical topics, including demonology, says, "A gift implies a settled and continued ability to do something again and again."[1] These gifts are not talents, Christian rules, or New Age Awareness. Though the gifts are meant to work together with the fruit of the Spirit so as to have a greater impact for God's glory, the gifts are not fruit of the Spirit. Appropriately developed in the Christian's life, these gifts should:

- Set you apart as a unique tool in God's hand,
- Affirm you as a believer,
- Involve you in what God is doing, and
- Bring you joy.

Six passages of Scripture list and clarify the gifts of the Holy Spirit: 1 Corinthians 12:1, 1 Corinthians 13:1–3, 1 Corinthians 14, Ephesians 4:11, 1 Peter 4:10–11, and Romans 12:4–10.

First Corinthians 12 emphasizes the diversity of the gifts in contrast to the unity of both the Holy Giver and the body of Christ when these gifts are applied biblically.

---

[1] Merrill Unger, *The Baptism & Gifts of the Holy Spirit* (Chicago: Moody Press, 1974), 139. Used by permission.

These verses list nine service and ministry gifts designed to foster spiritual health in the Church and to glorify God. First Corinthians 13 and 14 give additional information on the appropriate function and use of these gifts.

The gifts listed in Ephesians 4:11 are leadership gifts by which the saints are perfected, the work of the ministry is promoted, and the body of Christ is edified. First Peter 4:8–11 exhorts all Christians to charity in all that we do (reiterating the admonitions to charity in Romans 12:9–10 and 1 Corinthians 13) and to also provide willing hospitality, ministering as good stewards with the gifts God has given us.

The term "discerning of spirits" occurs in 1 Corinthians 12:10 as part of a list of gifts given by the Holy Spirit (vv. 4–11, emphasis is mine):

> Now there are diversities of gifts, but the same Spirit. And there are differences of administrations, but the same Lord. And there are diversities of operations, but it is the same God which worketh all in all. But the manifestation of the Spirit is given to every man to profit withal. For to one is given by the Spirit the word of wisdom; to another the word of knowledge by the same Spirit; to another faith by the same Spirit; to another the gifts of healing by the same Spirit; to another the working of miracles; to another prophecy; to another **discerning of spirits**; to another divers kinds of tongues; to another the inter-

pretation of tongues: But all these worketh
that one and the selfsame Spirit, dividing to
every man severally as he will.

In this passage, the Holy Spirit achieves a unity of
purpose and momentum through a diversity of gifts.

The Metaphor of the Human Body and God's Church

Romans 12:4–8 uses the metaphor of the human body
to demonstrate the necessity of the interactive nature of
the gifts of the Holy Spirit within the body of Christ,
His Church.

For as we have many members in one body,
and all members have not the same office:
so we, being many, are one body in Christ,
and every one members one of another.
Having then gifts differing according to the
grace that is given to us, whether prophecy,
let us prophesy according to the proportion
of faith; or ministry, let us wait on our ministering: or he that teacheth, on teaching; or
he that exhorteth, on exhortation: he that
giveth, let him do it with simplicity; he that
ruleth, with diligence; he that sheweth mercy,
with cheerfulness.

God uses the analogy of the body of Christ and the
organic unity achieved through the gifts given by God as
the biblical pattern for both the importance and function
of those gifts. In the same way that our human bodies

have different components based on cells that function in different ways as God created them to, the body of Christ has the components of the gifts of the Holy Spirit given by God to each believer. Even as our physical bodies cannot function properly if the components do not mature and function properly, so does God's Church fail to function properly and becomes unhealthy when Christians fail to use their spiritual gifts appropriately. The wise pastor and leadership team will direct those Christians willing to minister in their church into teams and ministries according to demonstrable spiritual gifts.

Keeping with the biblical model of the Church as the body of Christ (1 Corinthians 12), which requires all parts to be functional, it is reasonable to consider that God equips each local church with at least one person gifted to some extent in the discerning of spirits, which is the focus of this handbook.

About Discerning of Spirits

The gift of discerning of spirits is the ability to perceive beyond the physical/temporal world and to be aware of activity in the spiritual (invisible) realm, recognizing angelic and demonic interaction with each other and with the world of men. The purpose of this insight is to advance the Kingdom of God according to God's will and to provide protective information that can help His Church on earth.

People with this gift are often prayer warriors and may not understand all that they perceive if they are not adequately discipled or trained. As is true with all the gifts of the Spirit, a greater spiritual maturity and practice allows the Christian to use his or her unique gifts more effectively for the good of the whole body (1 Corinthians 12:7). The insight involved with the gift of discerning of spirits may range from the simple, internal prompt of a prayer warrior, to the presence of demonic activity or the actual perception of demons and what they are doing specifically to a person, church, or city (Acts 8:20–24).

Many Christians think that the gift of discerning of spirits denotes only the recognition of false teachers and their doctrines. However, the gift of discerning of spirits also involves the detection of spiritual activity leading to processes analogous to radar for spiritual warfare.

On the Pacific Coast, just south of the Klamath River inlet, there is a small farmhouse and barn located high above the rocky shore. It was used as a strategically placed and camouflaged radar station during World War II. Though hidden away and protected by the anonymity of their disguised position, the military operators of that station had the same basic training for combat readiness as their actively combatant military counterparts. Even today, radar and sonar operators continue to be necessary to modern warfare.

In the same way, those who are gifted in discerning of spirits act as radar for the protection and advanced warning of spiritual evil directed at both the Church and individual Christians. Just as physical military personnel need to be forewarned and fully armed for physical conflict, God's people need to have spiritual weapons and protections in place.[2]

This gift is more than the discernment of good and evil, which is biblically required of all Christians as they mature (Hebrews 5:15). The gift of discerning of spirits brings with it the ability to see, perceive, smell, sense, or be aware of the presence of both angels and demons. These sensations are baffling to the natural man and can be overwhelmingly disturbing to a person new to this gift. The experience of perceiving the spiritual realm defies normal human understanding of the sensory input from the physical world around us.

The Bible tells us there are satanic counterfeit expressions of this gift, often called clairvoyance.[3] There are ways to determine if the gift is authentically from God or not. The person with the authentic spiritual gift has to have received this ability to see or perceive the spiritual realm after their conversion to Christianity. Also, authentic experiences with this gift elicit godly responses, including praise of God, prayer, biblical counsel, exhortation, righteous action, and information given to the appropriate spiritual authority.

As a discerner of spirits matures in his or her understanding of God and of this gift, the ability to perceive the battle increases, corresponding with the ability to be

---

[2] See Chapter 5, "God's Provision for Victory in Warfare."
[3] See Chapter 13 for a more complete explanation of counterfeits of the gift of discerning of spirits.

an effective prayer warrior. Other results, like fear, anger, sin, doubt, estrangement from God, and alignment with the devil and his followers, are contrary to the use of this gift as a gift of the Holy Spirit. In this way, Satan, the destroyer and king of the Abyss (Revelation 9:11), would have a foothold to destroy the service of God by these means. Responses such as these bring into question the source of the occurrence, as well as the motives of the person demonstrating the alleged gift.

There is a great deal of misunderstanding regarding what the gift of discerning of spirits actually entails, largely because of the lack of instruction available about this gift. The Christians I asked to define the gift of discerning of spirits invariably answered that it was the discernment of false teachers and preachers. There is a distinction between the gift of discerning of spirits and what is typically called "discernment" in terms of false teachers and false prophets.

Discernment Versus Discerning of Spirits

While numerous biblical references use the word "discern" as a verb (see Hebrews 5:14) and "discerning" as a noun (see 1 Corinthians 12:10), there is nowhere in the Bible that mentions "discernment" as a spiritual gift. Instead, the accustomed usage for Christians is to state a mandated aspect of Christianity that is evident in the Bible in 1 John 4:1–3. While the passage makes no mention of the term itself, it alludes to the practice of discerning both false spirits and false prophets:

Beloved, believe not every spirit, but try the spirits whether they are of God: because many false prophets are gone out into the world. Hereby know ye the Spirit of God: Every spirit that confesseth that Jesus Christ is come in the flesh is of God: and every spirit that confesseth not that Jesus Christ is come in the flesh is not of God: and this is that spirit of antichrist, whereof ye have heard that it should come; and even now already is it in the world.

God directs us to know the Spirit of God and makes clear that we need to be able to distinguish the correct spirit behind the message in order to confirm that the message is indeed from God. He also makes it clear that this is not the discerning of false prophets and teachers but rather the discerning of spirits in general.

According to Ron Ovitt, basing his thoughts on 1 Corinthians 12:10, "Discernment means to be able to distinguish between right and wrong, good and evil. It is a logical, judicial ability to think through issues...the ability to discern whether a saying, teaching, doctrine, written word, or event is good or evil, true or false, and if the source, meaning, or intimations are of God, the person [who promotes the saying, teachings, etc.], or [if it is from] satanic deception. It is the ability to 'read between the lines' [and] to get to the truth of the issue. The 'gut' tells them something doesn't seem to be right.

There is an urgency to pray and ask for wisdom."[4] When the term "discernment" is used among Christians, this is generally what is meant.

The American Heritage Dictionary defines the word discernment as "to detect or perceive with the eye or the mind; to perceive distinctions of; to discriminate."[5]

John MacArthur calls discernment "...the skill of separating divine truth from error."[6] He continues to clarify with "First Thessalonians 5:21 says we are to 'examine everything carefully.'"[7] Second Thessalonians 2:3 also exhorts us to "let no man deceive you by any means."

The apostles exhort all Christians to spiritual maturity so we can tell the difference between good and evil (Ephesians 4:14; Hebrews 5:14). In order to achieve spiritual maturity, all Christians, no matter what spiritual gift God has given them, are called to "be not conformed to this world: but be ye transformed by the renewing of your mind, that ye may prove what is that good, and acceptable, and perfect, will of God" (Romans 12:2).

---

[4] Ronald Ovitt, *"Do You Have the Spiritual Gift of Discernment?"* (April 14, 2007), http://spiritualgifts.wordpress.com/2007/04/14/do-you-have-the-spiritual-gift-of-discernment/ [Accessed 3/13/2011]. Used by permission. Italics are added by this author.

[5] William Morris, ed., *The American Heritage Dictionary of the English Language* (New York: American Heritage Publishing Co., Inc. and Houghton Mifflin Company, 1971), 375.

[6] John MacArthur, "Discernment: Spiritual Survival for a Church in Crisis." *Grace to You.* Used by permission. http://www.gty.org/resources/positions/P02/discernment-spiritual-survival-for-a-church-in-crisis, n.d. [Accessed March 21, 2013].

[7] MacArthur, Ibid.

Christian author and film producer Caryl Matrisciana[8] and other Christians with whom I have spoken contend that all Christians have and should use the gift of discernment in this sense. There are numerous Bible references to wisdom. Pastor Gil Stieglitz of Principles to Live By relates that "being wise [as opposed to being foolish in Proverbs 14:18] is a discernment and filtering process."[9] The specific gift that is called "discernment"[10] gives certain people the ability to recognize the counterfeits more quickly.

While I agree with the necessity for the generalized vigilance that the Bible explicitly demands, there is also the implicit demonstration of perception of spiritual conflict that has been largely ignored in Western biblical teaching. In this sense, John Wimber and Kevin Springer's definition of discerning of spirits is more concise, "The discerning of spirits is the supernatural capacity to judge whether the motivating factor in a person is human, divine, or demonic. It is the supernatural insight into the source of spiritual activity."[11]

---

[8] Author and film producer Caryl Matrisciana has been led to expose the false teaching within evangelical churches resulting from New Age compromise and attempted unification with "all faiths." She has written a number of books and continues to produce films with subject matter covering not only heretical practices and preaching within the church but also current events as seen from a biblical worldview.

[9] Gil Stieglitz, "Principles to Live By" (email), July 20, 2007. Used by permission.

[10] Note the differentiation made between the terms "discernment" and "discerning of spirits." See Appendix 2 for the academic explanation of why I believe the difference is biblical.

[11] John Wimber with Kevin Springer, *Power Healing* (San Francisco: Harper Collins Publishers, 1987), 193. Used by permission.

Dr. Stieglitz contends that the present-day error is the focus on false prophets and teachers, but the recognition of false prophets and teachers is actually a side effect of the spiritual gift. Thus, the primary function of the spiritual gift of discerning of spirits is the recognition of evil spirits responsible for *both* the deception perpetrated by false teachers and the working of malevolent spiritual activity for other purposes of the Church.[12]

Summary

Whatever the Holy Spirit gifts us with, and whatever else God calls us to do with those gifts, He calls us to exercise those gifts with God's authority (1 Peter 4:10–11). Biblical reference to the gifts of the Holy Spirit presents the analogy of the body of Christ and the organic unity achieved through the gifts given by God as the biblical pattern for both the importance and function of those gifts.

The gift of the Holy Spirit called "discerning of spirits" is the ability to perceive beyond the physical and temporal world in which we live. The function of the discerner of spirits in the Church is like a radar operator for the military, recognizing spiritual activity with subsequent warning and information to be given to Church leaders. Just as the radar operator is not responsible for knowing what to do with the information or for leading the army into battle, the discerner of spirits is only

---

[12] Dr. Stieglitz expressed this view during a telephone conversation with me on September 9, 2013.

responsible for getting the information to those who need it in order to do the work God has called them to. The discerner of spirits also stands in the gap in prayer for both the Church and individuals, with intelligence gained from discernment events.

CHAPTER TWO

The Other Side of Discernment

Until recent decades, Christians in British and American cultures did not accept that demonism and overt spiritual warfare were real. For many years, missionaries have brought home stories of power encounters[1] with demons in foreign places that have been understood by their audiences as alien events happening elsewhere but with the perception that they have no direct impact locally on American Christians.

Spiritual Warfare Affects Everyone

When I was a child, I heard numerous missionary stories of shamans and witch doctors practicing their craft in attempts to destroy those sent to spread the gospel. The

---

[1] Edward F. Murphy. *The Handbook for Spiritual Warfare* (Nashville: Thomas Nelson, Inc., 2003), 540. "Power encounter" is defined as "a crisis point of encounter in the ongoing spiritual warfare between supernatural personages in which Christians are directly involved. Its goal is the glory of God, the defeat of the "no-gods" (Galatians 4:8–9), and the obedience of men to the one true God and His only begotten Son, the Lord Jesus Christ."

stories seemed far-fetched and tied only to culturally pagan people groups. When I served on a mission team in France, however, I came face to face with demonism in a supposedly "civilized" country. A person we shared the gospel with tried to physically attack a local pastor with extraordinary strength and in a way that was obviously outside human ability.

Although most Western Christians recognize the existence of spiritual warfare from a biblical perspective, the cultural tendency to separate the sacred (supernatural) from the secular (natural) disconnects Western believers from a personal understanding of spiritual warfare. Ed Murphy describes Western theology as being influenced by the naturalistic model of reality in which the universe is seen in terms of "cause-and-effect relationships between its constituent parts."[2]

Christians who have adopted this narrow worldview believe it is only in "pagan cultures" that Satan is still actively doing the things that the Bible portrays him doing. According to Timothy Warner, the assumption is that the natural and supernatural are separate with little apparent connection, and any physically apparent occurrence is not likely to be from the spiritual realm.[3]

Therefore, it is no surprise that Christians in Western churches have been taught that anything resembling the bizarre nature of the gift of discerning of spirits func-

---

[2] Murphy, Ibid., 4.
[3] Timothy Warner, *Spiritual Warfare: Victory Over the Powers of This Dark World* (Wheaton, IL: Crossway, 1991), 27. Used by permission.

tioning outside of prophecy and teaching is from the devil himself. Due to the lack of teaching on the true nature of spiritual warfare, any other application is understood within Christian circles as coming from the enemy, not from God.

Timothy Warner quotes Stanley Mooneyham's definition of discernment as the "recognition of spiritual conflict."[4] The gift of discerning of spirits encompasses applications beyond just recognizing false teachers and prophets. It also results in the exposure of spiritual activity and events that may or may not be related to prophecy and teaching. In describing those with the "righteous, Holy Spirit-given gift of discernment of spirits," Dr. Stieglitz uses the metaphor of the tools of war: "They are the radar and sonar for a spiritual war. Just as any physical war in modern times, station radar and sonar devices can tell of enemy troop movements, so in our spiritual war, people with the gifts of discernment of spirits can detect the movement of wicked spirits ... Many times I have been alerted to the work of the enemies through these God-placed sonar operators. We have then been able to prepare our church, myself, and others for the particular attack that is coming."[5]

Indeed, there has been a great deal of misunderstanding about this gift among Christians in the past. This is because so many Christians have embraced

---

[4] Warner, Ibid., 25.
[5] Gil Stieglitz, *Breaking Satanic Bondage: Intensive Training in Spiritual Warfare* (Roseville, CA: Principles to Live By, 2009), 100–101. Used by permission.

the Western worldview regarding the supernatural, as opposed to the natural, scientifically provable world. The existence of the "other side of discernment" is demonstrated by two sources of evidence:

- Implicit evidence of biblical accounts in both the Old and New Testaments, which demonstrate instances of spiritual perception or sightings, establishing the authority of this spiritual gift.

- Personal experiences of those with the gift and a mature assessment of its God-given, God-directed, and God-glorifying nature.

Old Testament Discerning of Spirits Events

Discerning of spirits is demonstrated throughout the Bible. A gift of the Holy Spirit, it was granted to certain believers in the New Testament. However, a number of references in the Old Testament imply the occasional granting of the gift of discerning of spirits for specific events and purposes. In Numbers 22, for instance, a beast of burden was given the ability to discern spirits for a short time when Balak, the king of Moab, demanded that Balaam curse the Israelites. God was angry because Balaam went with Balak contrary to His command.

He sent the angel of the LORD[6] to stop Balaam and his donkey (vv. 28–31). The animal was the first to see the

---

[6] The angel of the LORD is commonly understood to be "Christ in a pre-incarnate appearance." See William MacDonald, *Believers Bible Commentary Old Testament* (Nashville: Thomas Nelson Publishers, 1992), 191. This is also corroborated in the footnotes for this passage in *The King James Study Bible*. Liberty University, *The King James Study Bible* (Rio de Janeiro: Thomas Nelson, 1988), 269.

angel with the drawn sword and turned aside. Balaam became angry at the animal and struck her. The angel stood in front of the animal a second time, but this time between two walls so that Balaam's foot was crushed when the donkey turned to get away from the angel. The third time the angel stood in front of the animal, it was in a narrow place with no way to turn to the right or to the left. The donkey fell down under Balaam. You would think Balaam would have been astounded when the animal actually began to talk to him and complain about being struck three times.

After Balaam's threat to kill the animal, the donkey not only continued talking but also reasoned with him, reminding him of her faithful service as a beast of burden without complaint so far. God then opened Balaam's eyes and gave him a glimpse of the spiritual realm (discerning of spirits). He saw the angel of the LORD with the drawn sword, and the angel's rebuke brought Balaam to a dubious repentance.[7] Balaam did bless Israel in the end, but he did so unwillingly. His actions appeared to come exclusively from fear, instead of loving reverence for God, as he lamented that there is "no enchantment against Jacob, neither is there any divination against Israel" (Numbers 23:23).

---

[7] Second Peter 2 describes how false teachers distort the truth, live ungodly lives, and draw the unwary into error and sin. Verses 15 and 16 bring Balaam into the discussion, portraying him as one "who loved the wages of unrighteousness." Further indication of his status as an unbeliever is found in verse 17. The context of this verse seems to include him in the final condemnation to hell of such people: "These are wells without water, clouds carried with a tempest; to whom the mist of darkness is reserved forever."

Further evidence in the Old Testament of ability like the New Testament gift of discerning of spirits occurred when the king of Syria warred against Israel. The king of Israel had been able to avoid Syria's battle attempts numerous times. In 2 Kings 6, Syria's king wondered who had betrayed him and informed the king of Israel of Syria's plans. The king of Syria was told that it was Elisha, the prophet, who "telleth the king of Israel the words that thou speakest in thy bedchamber" (v. 12). In response, the king of Syria sent "horses, and chariots, and a great host" to surround and take the city of Dothan where Elisha was staying.

Elisha's servant fearfully told his master of the situation. Elisha answered, "Fear not: for they that be with us are more than they that be with them" (v. 16). Elisha then called upon God to enable his servant to see that "the mountain was full of horses and chariots of fire round about Elisha" (v. 17). It appears that Elisha knew practical help was already there and he could probably see the army sent from heaven. What he saw was either an open window (momentary glimpse) from the physical world into the spiritual world, or an intrusion of the supernatural into the natural world by the heavenly host.[8]

Elisha's ability to discern spirits was a result of his unbroken communion with God[9] who allowed him to

---

[8] See chapters 7 through 12 for a more complete explanation of the experience of the gift of discerning of spirits.

[9] Two public miracles in 2 Kings 2:19–24 establish Elisha's succession to Elijah's ministry: the healing of the water in Jericho and the cursing of the children who mocked him. In addition, he is given the moniker of "the man of God" numerous times, the first of which is in 2 Kings 4:7.

see as if the soldiers were physical beings and without having to ask for it[10] (vv. 15–17). At Elisha's request, his servant was also able to "see," and they both rejoiced over the recognition of the supernatural presence granted by God's authority in direct answer to prayer.

Another instance occurred in 1 Chronicles 21:16, when David was given sight of an angel poised in the sky above Jerusalem with an outstretched sword. God sent the angel to destroy the Israelites with pestilence in response to David's disobedience when he took a census contrary to God's declared will. God relented and stopped the angel of destruction above the threshing floor of Ornan the Jebusite. Years later, the Temple was built on this site in Jerusalem. The Bible does not record that the men with David (elders of Israel) also saw the angel. This appears to have been a spiritually discerned event given exclusively to David.

In Daniel 3, when King Nebuchadnezzar saw the fourth person "like the Son of God"[11] in verse 25, he was likely experiencing discerning of spirits. Again, the possibility of either a momentary glimpse of a spiritual event or an intrusion of the spiritual realm into the physical world occurred. If it was the Lord Jesus Christ in a pre-incarnate physical form (the angel of

---

[10] Nothing indicates that Elisha asked to see God's provision, but that doesn't mean he did not pray for the protection or for the revelation of the protection.

[11] *The King James Study Bible* footnote indicates that "Nebuchadnezzar had no knowledge of Christ and was probably saying nothing more than that a divine being was protecting the three men. The fourth person may have been the pre-incarnate Christ, who often appears in the Old Testament as 'the angel of the LORD,' or may have been an angel sent by God to protect the men." Liberty University, *The King James Study Bible*, 1276.

the LORD), then this might have been either sight or discerning of spirits. However, if it were an angel or non-physical appearance of the Lord, then Nebuchadnezzar would have been granted "discerning of spirits" in seeing the spiritual manifestation of God's protection for Shadrach, Meshach, and Abednego. Either way, the result was an acknowledgment of the power of God.

In the book of Daniel, chapter 10 also records an incident of "discerning of spirits" in that Daniel was the only one who saw the strange man who came in answer to Daniel's fasting and prayer. The man's supernatural appearance, attire, and voice set him apart as being otherworldly. He informed Daniel that he had been hindered by the prince of the kingdom of Persia from coming those twenty-one days of Daniel's vigil until the Archangel Michael had come to help him. Only then was he able to bring his message to Daniel.

In that same passage, the men who were with Daniel "saw not the vision; but a great quaking fell upon them, so that they fled to hide themselves" (v. 7). While they did not actually see the messenger, they recognized that there was a spiritual event taking place around them; this is also a form of discerning of spirits. Unable to know how to interpret or understand the occurrence, they hid because they were afraid.

New Testament Discerning of Spirits Events

While the words "discerning of spirits" as a spiritual gift are used only once in the Bible, in 1 Corinthians

12:10, the gift is frequently present in the New Testament by implication. During His life on earth, Jesus Himself demonstrated all the gifts listed in 1 Corinthians 12,[12] Romans 12, Ephesians 4, and 1 Peter 4.

In Matthew 4:1–11, Jesus practiced "discerning of spirits" when He recognized and reprimanded Satan for trying to ensnare Him. Jesus also knew that Satan was behind Peter's words in Matthew 16:22–23, exercising "discernment" in the sense that He recognized false teaching.

The deliverance of the two demoniacs in the country of the Gergesenes in Matthew 8 required a "discerning of spirits"[13] so that appropriate action could be taken. This instance of spiritual warfare appears to be the same as the case of the Gadarene demoniac, found in Mark 5 and Luke 8. Jesus recognized the presence of the legion of spirits and commanded them to go into the herd of swine nearby. Additionally, Luke 22:31 tells us that Jesus demonstrated both prophetic and spiritual insight

---

[12] The spiritual gift of tongues is possibly the exception. There is no explicit mention of Jesus using "tongues" in the New Testament. Only by deduction can it be said that, in as cosmopolitan a society as He lived, He could have spoken to anyone and been understood in his or her own language. However, that it is not stated in the New Testament is notable. In Matthew 13:54–56, His neighbors were surprised at His wisdom and knowledge. In Luke 4:16, He read from Isaiah, an act indicative of enough education to know how to read if He were just a man. It would have been a miraculous, extraordinary event for a largely uneducated carpenter's son to be fluent enough in another language to be understood. But then Jesus is God and capable of much more than a mere man would be able to do.

[13] Although the demons gave themselves away when they cried out, "What have we to do with thee, Jesus, thou son of God? Art thou come hither to torment us before the time?" (Matthew 8:29).

because He knew Peter would be "sifted" by Satan[14] and that Peter would fail the test by denying his Lord.

The apostles and disciples also demonstrated the gift of discerning of spirits. Before He sent them out on their first mission, Jesus empowered His disciples with authority over all demons and to heal "all manner of sickness and disease" (Matthew 10:1, 8; Luke 9:1). They even cast out demons in Jesus's name (Mark 6:13). This spiritual warfare is where the discerning of spirits gift is so very important for Christians, even today. In order to determine that there were indeed demons to deal with in any given situation, the disciples had to exercise discerning of spirits. Luke 10:17 documents that "the seventy returned again with joy, saying, 'Lord, even the devils are subject unto us through thy name.'"

Discerning of spirits does not always have to do with evil spirits, as we have seen in the Old Testament sightings of angels. Acts 12 cites the story of Peter's imprisonment by Herod. An angel came to release him, leaving the two soldiers asleep who had been charged with guarding him. Allowed by God to see the angel, Peter thought it was a vision.

At first, the people who were praying for Peter did not believe the miracle of his release. They were so surprised at the answered prayer they thought it was his ghost that had arrived at their door. Happily, they were

---

[14] Luke 22:31 is not the first time in the Bible that Satan has asked permission to go after God's people. In Job chapters 1 and 3, Satan is given permission to test Job within the boundary of his life.

mistaken. God still had more for His beloved disciple to do in this life.

Peter also discerned the activity of the devil when he confronted Ananias and Sapphira for lying about their donation in Acts 5:1–11. He asked specifically, "Why has Satan filled your heart to lie to the Holy Ghost?"

Likewise, Paul used "discerning of spirits" in his work. In Acts 16:16–18, he recognized that it was a demonic spirit of divination that prompted the girl to cry out, "These men are the servants of the most high God, which [show] us the way of salvation."[15] The outcome was spiritual warfare in which Paul commanded the spirit to leave her in Jesus's name.

Enough information is recorded in the New Testament to give us solid doctrine, but not every single incident in the lives of Jesus or His disciples is written there. Hence, it would follow that these were not the only occurrences of discerning of spirits in the lives of Jesus or of the disciples. They are simply representative examples of the *prerogative of authority and expectation over demonic power in Jesus's name* given to us in the New Testament (Matthew 10:1, 28:18–20; Luke 9:1).

In his first letter, John recognized the need to use "discernment" as part of a maturing Christian's parameters of growth and service. He cited false prophets in the world as an example when he exhorted his readers

---

[15] Though she told the truth, the girl must have done so in a derogatory and disruptive way for Paul to have been bothered by her repeated pronouncements.

to "*test* the spirits" in 1 John 4:1. The purpose of John's letter appears to assure his readers of their salvation "that your joy may be full" (v. 4). Therefore, it follows that he would warn them about anyone who was "not of God" so that "hereby know we the spirit of truth, and the spirit of error" (v. 6). It also follows that he would give them the tools to determine the origin of the spirits they were to test.

Several pastors I spoke to said that if they are uncertain about the spiritual status of someone they encounter, they ask, "What do you think of Jesus?" At times, this question has caused the ones asked to become ill at ease, even to the point of fleeing the scene. The very name of Jesus is powerful enough to cause the enemy of our souls and his servants to take flight. One pastor further pointed out that demons recognize us as discerners of spirits and can't easily tolerate our presence.

Differentiated Consequences

Notice the difference between discernment of spirits that are not of God, as in identifying false teaching in 1 John 4, and the gift of "discerning of spirits," as in recognizing and commanding the demons in Jesus's name. First John 4 applies to both knowing the spirit behind the message and recognizing when spirits are not of God. "Discerning of spirits" pertaining to spiritual warfare (commanding evil spirits to leave, for example) does not occur in the same ways as in situations in which spiritual counterfeits are present in the message.

The spirits behind false prophets and teachers have not been commanded to leave, whereas the spirits discovered in "discerning of spirits" were dealt with severely by both Jesus (Matthew 8:32) and the disciples (Acts 16:18). Perhaps this is because false teachings are primarily demon-influenced, and therefore require aspects of church discipline ending in "excommunication"[16] if there is no repentance. But the demoniacs requiring spiritual warfare for deliverance involve full-blown demonic possession.

Satan's endgame is to attempt to duplicate and cloud spiritual issues for his purposes. The Temptation of Christ in Matthew 4 is the most prominent biblical example of this. Satan uses Scripture, the Word of God, to try to defeat the human Jesus with false teaching. Being the Messiah, God incarnate, Jesus does not fall to the temptations that Satan throws at Him. Instead, He uses Scripture correctly to refute the enemy and tells him to go away.

This is spiritual warfare, the battle for the will and mind of an individual. Using warfare terminology, it is an offensive assault deflected by a corresponding defensive quoting of Scripture. It is unlike spiritual warfare in which a direct command sends demons scurrying away from a stronghold. That the perpetrator of the

---

[16] Matthew 18 describes the steps in dealing with in-church discipline. Once the false teacher/prophet is no longer considered a Christian, he is treated as if he or she is a "heathen" and the issue could conceivably become one of "discerning of spirits" (i.e., taking action as for full-blown demon possession in an unbeliever).

attack is Satan himself, who appears to have had access on demand to God's Royal Court,[17] could explain the difference in part. But this event happened before Jesus sacrificed His life on the cross and then took it up again. Jesus Christ's death, burial, and resurrection were God's once-for-all victory over Satan and his demons on behalf of all creation. The Bible is clear that believers already partake of this victory over Satan, and indeed, they have been given authority in Jesus's name to command him and his demons away.

The gift of discerning of spirits, like the other spiritual gifts, is sometimes granted to those who are normally not endowed with that particular gift for apparently event-specific reasons. In Luke 5:8, for instance, Peter is given insight (discerning of spirits) to recognize Jesus as Lord. The Greek term used here is *kurios*, which means "supreme in authority."[18] He had witnessed the miracle of the vast number of fish caught when Jesus had told him and his coworkers to throw their nets. He identified Jesus's divine nature to be the source of that miracle. This incident indicates there is a function of the gift of discerning of spirits in salvation.

Later in Luke 5 and the following chapters, the scribes and Pharisees observed many miracles as well, like the disciples and others who followed Jesus; however, they did not recognize Jesus as Messiah, Savior, and Lord.

---

[17] See Job 1 and 2.

[18] James Strong, *Strong's Exhaustive Concordance of the Bible Together with Dictionaries of the Hebrew and Greek Words of the Original* (MacDonald Publishing Company, n.d.), 44.

They simply continued questioning everything Jesus and His disciples did. For the most part, they lacked the faith to understand the spiritual significance of the answers and so were not permitted the spiritual vision, a form of discerning of spirits, to accept Jesus as Lord and Savior.[19]

Since we are warned so frequently in the New Testament about false prophets and apostles, by implication then, "discernment" and the maturity necessary to employ it is not a specific spiritual gift granted to a few, but it is required of all those who belong to Christ. For example, 1 Timothy 1:3–4 includes warnings on listening to fables and genealogies, as well as doctrine other than what has been given by God. First Timothy 6:3–5 requires that we withdraw ourselves from those who produce strife and division with their meaningless babble:

> If any man teach otherwise, and consent not to wholesome words, even the words of our Lord Jesus Christ, and to the doctrine which is according to godliness; he is proud, knowing nothing, but doting about questions and strifes of words, whereof cometh envy, strife, railings, evil surmisings, perverse disputings of men of corrupt minds, and destitute of the truth, supposing that gain is godliness: from such withdraw thyself.

---

[19] Ephesians 2:7–9 indicates that even the faith to accept Jesus Christ as Lord and Savior is a gift from God.

Discernment of false doctrine and those who preach it is based on the fruit of the purveyor of deception. Jesus Himself gave us this standard in Matthew 7:16–20:

> Ye shall know them by their fruits. Do men gather grapes of thorns, or figs of thistles? Even so every good tree bringeth forth good fruit; but a corrupt tree bringeth forth evil fruit. A good tree cannot bring forth evil fruit, neither can a corrupt tree bring forth good fruit. Every tree that bringeth not forth good fruit is hewn down, and cast into the fire. Wherefore by their fruit ye shall know them.

Second Timothy 3:9 also tells us that "their folly shall be manifest unto all men,"[20] and 1 John 4 presents the lack of confession of Jesus Christ come in the flesh as the distinguishing feature of the spirit of antichrist behind false prophecy. The decisive factor is always the Word of God: "Study to shew thyself approved unto God, a workman that needeth not to be ashamed, rightly dividing the word of truth" (2 Timothy 2:15).

Both direct and indirect biblical instructions about discernment and the gift of discerning of spirits continue to be even more relevant to today's born-again believers than they were when they were first given. Throughout

---

[20] Regarding the preceding verse, "Now as Jannes and Jambres withstood Moses, so do these also resist the truth," the footnote in *The King James Study Bible* (p. 1900) says that, "Jannes and Jambres, according to Jewish tradition, were the two magicians in Pharaoh's court, who attempted to duplicate Moses's miracles." The entire passage relates to seeking for truth outside God's Word, mere religion without the power of God.

the world, Satan continues to do his worst against Christians, frequently using subtlety to veil his actions. But in the world beyond the church doors, his actions are no longer veiled, even in America. Since Jesus Christ won the final victory against the devil on the cross, one is left to wonder why Satan is allowed continued access to God, influence over world affairs, and apparent success impacting Christian lives.

Summary

There are two sides to the spiritual gift of discernment involved in the protection of God's Church. The same mechanism (supernatural recognition of spiritual warfare generated by the presence of satanic forces) is incorporated for both, but different outcomes exist for each:

- The recognition of false teaching and false prophecy through the spiritual gift of discernment, which is present to some extent in all mature Christians, creates a response of prayer with exhortation and correction as the outcome.

- The recognition of spiritual conflict using the spiritual gift of discerning of spirits engenders prayer and action in the sense of actively "standing in the gap" against satanic and demonic attacks. It also gives advanced warning of danger to the Church and participates in activities related to spiritual warfare, both during and outside of church meetings, including the provision of information for deliverance procedures.

CHAPTER THREE

The Beginning of Spiritual Warfare

Spiritual warfare began before human existence and was initiated when Lucifer coveted God's position. When God created the angels, He created them holy and righteous. Some very high-ranking ones guarded His throne and His glory. Ezekiel 28 cites angelic positional information regarding Lucifer, who became jealous and covetous of God's glory, wanting to usurp it for himself.

The Fall of Lucifer

Although there is no record of the events preceding this incident, the reasons for his fall are clearly stated. Isaiah 14:12–14 reveals that Lucifer, "son of the morning," has fallen from heaven because,

> … thou hast said in thine heart, I will ascend to heaven, I will exalt my throne above the stars of God: I will sit also upon the mount

of the congregation ... I will ascend above the heights of the clouds; I will be like the most High.

In addition, Jesus tells of having seen "Satan as lightning fall from heaven" in Luke 10:18. Satan was hurled down for his arrogance and disobedience. He invaded the "fair Earth" of God's creation, and history became the story of Satan's efforts to thwart God's plans. Satan himself continued to act on these goals when he tempted Jesus in the wilderness (Matthew 4:9). However, since "a created being cannot rise to a level higher than that for which he was created by God ... Satan's domain [of degradation] today is more likely the evidence of his failure rather than the realization of his purpose."[1] Instead of achieving God's glory for himself, Lucifer has become the epitome of what is *un*godly.

Some view Satan as the opposite of God. Nevertheless, since God created Lucifer as an angel, Satan cannot be the opposite of the one who created him. C. S. Lewis cites him specifically as the opposite of Michael, the Archangel, only in the sense that a bad man is the opposite of a good man (i.e., the depravity of Satan contrasted with the righteous obedience of Michael.) However, Satan continues to be a very powerful angel, like Michael, though Lucifer became corrupted by his own choice. Demons who followed Lucifer in his rebellion "by the abuse of their free will, have become ene-

---

[1] Warner, *Spiritual Warfare*, 17.

mies of God and, as a corollary, to us."[2] Lucifer is now called "the devil," which means "slanderer," and he is the "adversary" written about in 1 Peter 5:8, "Be sober, be vigilant; because your adversary the devil, as a roaring lion, walketh about, seeking whom he may devour."

Evil is not just an immaterial standard by which we judge what happens around us. The Bible indicates that a hunger to overpower and absorb all is the primary craving of the evil one and his minions. Biblical incidents of demonic possession clearly demonstrate the apparently all-consuming nature of the spirits in possession, leaving nothing of the host free to express anything from their own person. C. S. Lewis opined that Satan's "dream is of the day when all shall be inside him, and all that says 'I' can say it only through him. This, I surmise, is the bloated-spider parody, the only imitation he can understand, of that unfathomed bounty whereby God turns tools into servants and servants into sons, so that they may be at last reunited to Him in the perfect freedom of a love offered from the height of the utter individualities which He has liberated them to be."[3] It is no coincidence that those who are deceived by the so-called "Eastern Religions" cite their goal in life to be "one with the universe." This is Satan's perversion of God's perfect will for humanity.

---

[2] C. S. Lewis, *The Best of C. S. Lewis* (Grand Rapids, MI: Baker Book House, 1977), 4. The excerpt is from the preface to *The Screwtape Letters*.
[3] Lewis, *The Best of C. S. Lewis*, 9.

Numerous Bible references show Satan standing in the presence of God. Zechariah 3:1 specifically states that Satan stands at the right hand of the angel of the Lord "to resist him." In Revelation 12:10 he is called "the accuser of our brethren," and we learn from this verse that he is continually ("day and night") doing so in God's presence.[4] Mark Bubeck explains, "Satan's desire is to cause us to condemn ourselves. He wants to cause a believer to have vagueness about what he has done wrong and seeks to keep him from knowing what to do about his sin. This is opposite to the conviction of the Holy Spirit. The Holy Spirit convicts us of definite sins and shows us that through the shed blood of Christ there is cleansing and forgiveness."[5]

And yet, Ezekiel 28:12–19 (ESV) describes the beauty and high position of Lucifer in God's royal court before his downfall. The passage begins with a lament for the king of Tyre. However, the description of the king, "You were the signet of perfection, full of wisdom and perfect in beauty … You were blameless in your ways from the day you were created" (vv. 12b, 15), is not that of a human. F. C. Jennings points out, "of no child of Adam could this be said."[6] The only human who is perfect is Jesus Himself, whose perfection made His redemptive act of sacrifice on the cross possible.

---

[4] "… for the accuser of our brethren is cast down, which accused them before our God day and night" (Revelation 12:10b).
[5] Mark Bubeck, *The Adversary: The Christian Versus Demonic Activity* (Chicago: Moody Bible Institute, 1975), 58. Used by permission.
[6] F. C. Jennings, *Satan: His Person, Work, Place, and Destiny* (New York: Loiseaux Brothers, n.d.), 52.

It has been suggested that Lucifer was the first being created by God.[7] His name means "Light Bearer" (Isaiah 14:12), and he has now become "an angel of light" to deceive even the children of God (2 Corinthians 11:14).[8] Ezekiel 28:16 specifies that his purpose in heaven was that of "covering cherub." Jennings suggests that the cherubim "represent God to the world" as an image on a coin represents the government that minted it.[9] The use of the designation "cherub" for Satan in Ezekiel 28 "in itself at once suggests to us that his office was in connection with the government or throne of God; and further, that it was to maintain inviolate the righteousness of that throne."[10]

The symbolism of the cherubim guarding the mercy seat on the Ark of the Covenant is not lost here. The figures on the ark, as described in Exodus 25:19–20, "stretch out their wings on high, covering the mercy seat with their wings." The mercy seat on the ark was "the place where God abode on earth."[11] Just as the cherubim guarded the mercy seat on earth, so too the heavenly cherubim cover the throne of God "in order to protect

---

[7] Gregory Kuehn, "Terrorist Intel, Part 2," Sierra Bible Church, September 26, 2010, Reno, Nevada. Pastor Greg Kuehn points out that the designation "son of the morning (dawn)" gives the impression that Lucifer was God's first created being.

[8] Preceding verses (2 Corinthians 11:1–13) describe scenarios of false teaching ending with the fact that false teachers "transform themselves into the apostles of Christ. And no marvel; for Satan himself is transformed into an angel of light." Galatians 1:8–9 reiterates the warnings of 2 Corinthians that if anyone, even "an angel from heaven, preach any other gospel unto you than that which we have preached unto you, let him be accursed."

[9] Jennings, *Satan: His Person, Work, Place, and Destiny*, 40.

[10] Jennings, Ibid., 41.

[11] Jennings, Ibid., 42.

that throne from anything that might shake its foundations."[12] As Psalm 89:14a (ESV) says, "Righteousness and justice are the foundation of Your throne."

Jennings presents a word picture of the foundation of righteousness of the throne (justice and judgment) with the throne itself (the mercy seat) on top.[13] The perfect balance between mercy and righteousness must be protected at all cost in that "The slightest reversal of perfect righteousness of any character, either on the side of punishment of the just or mercy to the guilty, overturns the throne and its foundations are destroyed."[14]

Lucifer, then, was created to be the guardian of righteousness and mercy (of which the seats are metaphorical images) of God,[15] a high position from which to fall indeed. The presence of such protection does not predicate the actual presence of disorder, rebellion, or sin. The Kingdom of God is in perfect order, and each of the cherubim was created in varying ranks, delegated to maintain that perfection.[16]

---

[12] Jennings, Ibid., 52.
[13] "Justice and Judgment are the habitation of thy throne" (Psalm 89:14a) and "Thy throne is upholden by mercy" (Prov 20:28).
[14] Jennings, *Satan: His Person, Work, Place, and Destiny*, 43–44.
[15] Jennings, Ibid., 128.
[16] Jennings, Ibid., 44.

Satan's Desire to Defy God

When God created Adam and Eve, He gave them dominion over all the earth (Genesis 1:26). When Adam and Eve disobeyed God's command to not eat of the tree of the knowledge of good and evil, they subjugated themselves (and all of earth, which God had given them to rule) under Satan's dominion. In other words, by sinning, they gave up to Satan the position of authority that God had given to them.

"So complete and final was Adam's authority over the earth that he, not just God, had the ability to give it away to another!"[17] Satan, the fallen Lucifer, is now designated as the "prince of this world" (John 12:31), "prince of the power of the air"[18] (Ephesians 2:2), and "the god of this world" (2 Corinthians 4:4), who blinds the minds of unbelievers and leads the world into disobedience to God. In addition, he is called the "wicked one" (Matthew 13:38), "destroyer" (Revelation 9:11), "the dragon" (Revelation 12:7), a murderer and liar (John 8:44), all designating additional facets of his actions on earth.

Isaiah 14:13–14 tells us that Lucifer, "son of the morning" (v. 12), wanted to assume the Messianic and positional promises given to our Lord Jesus Christ.

---

[17] Dutch Sheets, *Intercessory Prayer: How God Can Use Your Prayers to Move Heaven and Earth* (Ventura, CA: Regal/Gospel Light, 1996), 29.
[18] He is also called "Beelzebub" in Matthew 12:24, and the "prince of the devils" in Matthew 9:34, 12:24, and Mark 3:22. He is also called "prince of this world" in John 12:31, 14:30, and 16:11.

His first desire was to go into heaven, an act done only with God's permission. In addition, Jesus was the first to ascend into heaven, taking with Him all those waiting in Paradise through the ages for that very moment (Ephesians 4:8–10). Satan's desire, then, was to usurp Jesus's place.[19] Satan is permitted access to God, and, for now, he accuses the brethren to God day and night (Revelation 12:10). But because Jesus paid the blood price for our sins on the cross, Satan cannot act against the children of God without permission from God. Although Satan has access, he no longer has authority before the throne of God.

The second and third desires were to "exalt my throne above the stars of God ... [and] sit on the mount of the congregation, in the sides of the north" (Isaiah 14:13). Since the fall of Lucifer apparently took place before the creation of humans on earth,[20] these refer to spiritual realms, not physical geography. These are also attempts to usurp God's authority, which rightfully belongs to Jesus (Colossians 1:16). Based on the context of pre-terrestrial events, "stars of God" in this passage indicate something other than stars that shine at night; therefore, the goal would have been to rule over the spirit world in its entirety and to do so with unchallenged authority. The term "mount" and its variations are men-

---

[19] Kuehn, Terrorist Intel, Part 2.
[20] Jennings suggests that the cataclysm that rendered the earth "without form and void" in Genesis 1:2 accompanied the fall of Lucifer. See pages 70–73 of *Satan: His Person, Work, Place, and Destiny* for the full explanation.

tioned in the Old Testament many times;[21] the context is connected to an act of governance and authority. For example, Ezekiel 28:16 describes Lucifer's removal from "the mountain of God"; that is, away from the center of universal authority and power.

In context, "the sides of the north" connects to a congregation outside of Israel. This also refers to the spiritual realm of God's Kingdom since Satan's rebellion evidently came before the creation of humans and the existence of Israel.[22] Since he is already called the "prince of the power of the air" (Ephesians 2:2) and, as such, already has access to physical space around the earth, the statement "I will ascend above the heights of the clouds" has to do with spiritual places in the "heavens" more than the physical stratosphere. Finally, "I will be like the most High" clearly demonstrates Lucifer's craving for supreme power to replace God.

The Results of Satan's Rebellion

The results of these desires were Satan's loss of God's favor and banishment from heaven with his followers, a third of God's angels (Revelation 12:4), who were deceived by Lucifer's lies. Except for the occasions when he is allowed into God's presence by divine permission, Satan appears to be bound to the earth in his wanderings (Job 1:7; 1 Peter 5:8–9), controlling those who are

---

[21] Examples are Mount Sinai, Mount Horeb, Mount Ephraim, and Mount Zion.
[22] The presence of Satan in the garden of Eden so soon after the creation of the world points to the pre-existence of evil, hence the concept of Satan's fall taking place before the creation of humans and the garden they were to tend.

spiritually lost while rousing all people to sin (Genesis 3:1–6; 1 John 5:19). His power appears to be restricted to the terrestrial sphere and restrained only by the will of God (Job 1:10–12). Yet he is able to oppose other high-ranking angels who, understanding his great power, decline to censure him, referring him instead to ultimate rebuke, God's reprimand (Daniel 10:12–13; Jude 1:9).

Besides accusing believers day and night, he harasses them with affliction and disease (Acts 10:38; 2 Corinthians 12:7), ensnaring both the wicked and the justified with evil thoughts and deeds (John 13:2; Acts 5:3; 1 Timothy 3:7). According to Mark Bubeck, "with Christians [Satan] delights to play both ends against the middle. As the tempter, he delights to inject into our minds wicked thoughts and desires. Then, as the accuser, he loves to taunt us about what a terrible person we are to have such wicked and sinful thoughts as those."[23]

Satan's goal of deceiving even the children of God involves both the use of false teachers among them (Matthew 13:39) and the restriction of comprehension of spiritual matters. The Parable of the Sower in Mark 4:15 directs attention to his ability to even take "away the word that was sown in their hearts," hindering any kind of understanding of the Word of God. Other forms of satanic abuse include preventing God's servants from carrying out their divinely appointed business (1 Thessalonians 2:18) and casting God's people into prison (Revelation 2:10).

---

[23] Bubeck, *The Adversary*, 71. Used by permission.

Only able to imitate (not reproduce) God's power, Satan's "parodies" of the forms of God's interaction with the world and its human inhabitants are deeply flawed. His obsession with consuming all those about him fuels religious ideals of being one with the universe. The falsehood of devotion to these beliefs falls right into his design to deceive and take all he can from the Kingdom of God, even to the point of deceiving Christians. The enemy and his demons can also influence actions by entering and controlling an unsaved person (John 13:27).

But thanks be to God, Jesus was triumphant on the cross over all of Satan's challenges, including his power of death and the resultant fear of death. Hebrews 2:14–15 tells us:

> Forasmuch then as the children are partakers of flesh and blood, he also himself likewise took part of the same; that through death he might destroy him that had the power of death, that is, the devil; and deliver them who through fear of death were all their lifetime subject to bondage.

Unbelievers remain in that bondage, but believers are free of that bondage of fear and are free to choose righteousness in Christ. Because of His victory, Christians are not subject to "possession" but can still be *influenced*, even oppressed, by the devil through the world and the flesh. Edward Murphy calls this "demonic attachment" or "demonization."[24]

---

[24] Murphy, *Handbook for Spiritual Warfare*, 508.

Clinical case studies presented in Fred Dickason's *Demon Possession and the Christian* seem to indicate that a Christian can be controlled by demons in the same way as an unbeliever. However, the preponderance of examples of counseling and deliverance sessions where Christians were found to be demon-controlled seems to point to pre-conversion infestation. Dickason cites the instance of Alice who was possessed by a demon called "Non-acceptance" in childhood before she knew Christ as her Savior. This demon had further initiated access for other demons to inhabit her.

Another client, Burt, had been a psychic before he accepted Jesus as his Savior. His original demon possession had also occurred early in life. The number of demons was added to during a laying-on-of-hands event as a result of his request to receive the gift of tongues. This kind of invasion from tongues-related events seems to be a common theme in deliverance scenarios with Christians. Dickason suggests that many times, tongues are a manifestation of demonic activity, a serious counterfeit of the gift that was demonstrated at Pentecost.

Carla had actually experienced a pact with the devil before her conversion. The demonic presence activated in the form of harassment after she became a Christian and began to grow in the Lord. Again, post-conversion, laying on of hands with the purpose of achieving the gift of tongues led to the addition of more opportunistic demons to the layers of existing evil spirits. All three were delivered from their tormentors, but only after exhaustive self-examination, repentance, confession, and power prayer.

Fred Dickason addressed the controversial nature of the issue of the relationship of demons to Christians with the statement, "We recognize the lack of conclusive evidence in the Bible on this issue and would not elevate our [experience-based] conclusion to the stature of biblical truth. But we have found the factual [experiential] truth to be that Christians can be and have been demonized."[25]

While it is true that there is not one chapter and verse we can point to that definitively shows a Christian can or cannot be "demonized" (i.e., possessed after conversion), Scripture clearly implies the concept of satanic influence in the life of a Christian. If Satan could not get a foothold in the lives of Christians, for instance, then why are we warned about it? In Ephesians, Christians are instructed how to live now that "we belong to the Lord." Ephesians 4:27 specifies that we "neither give place to the devil." Jim Logan makes the point that the word translated "place" in this verse "is the Greek word *topos* … It's the root of English words like topography, and refers to the ground or a specific spot or location."[26]

---

[25] Fred Dickason, *Demon Possession and the Christian: A New Perspective* (Chicago: Moody Publishers, 1987), 157.
[26] Jim Logan, *Reclaiming Surrendered Ground* (Chicago: Moody Publishers, 1995), 33. Used by permission.

In spiritual warfare terms, the word *topos* signifies a "point of attachment."[27] According to Clinton Arnold, "It is likely that any sinful activity that the believer does not deal with by the power of the Holy Spirit can be exploited by the Devil and turned into a means of control over the believer's life. Therefore, Christians need to resist.

"For Paul there is no middle ground. There is no nominal Christianity. Believers either resist the influence of the Evil One, who works through the flesh and the world, or they relinquish control of their lives to the power of darkness. Giving in to those temptations does not confirm the weakness of the flesh; it opens up the lives of believers to the control of the devil and his powers. We need to recognize the supernatural nature of temptation and be prepared to face it."[28]

While Jesus has already prevailed over Satan (Matthew 12:22–29), Satan's defeat is ongoing in that he continues to resist. With the knowledge of his approaching execution (Revelation 12:12,17), he and his demons continue to do as much damage to humans as they can, especially to Christians. He is sovereign over his own kingdom (Matthew 12:26; Luke 11:14–18), complete with his own "throne" (Revelation 2:13) and "congregation" (Revelation 2:9).

---

[27] Dr. Stieglitz expressed this view during a telephone conversation with me on September 9, 2013.

[28] Clinton Arnold, *The Powers of Darkness* (Downers Grove, IL: Intervarsity, 1992), 128.

Christ's redemptive act on the cross not only redeemed us from our sin, but it also redeemed us from the *authority* of the devil. Throughout the New Testament, Christians are called to stand against this foe and are equipped through the Holy Spirit and Scripture to do battle against him without fear even of death[29] (Colossians 2:10–15). That calling includes both an understanding of the spiritual warfare in which we participate and the use of the spiritual gifts that God has given each of us. Discerning of spirits is only one of them, yet it is particularly important because it is so very specific to the evil campaign against humanity.

Summary

The very nature of spiritual warfare is the evidence for the necessity of the gift of discerning of spirits. Satan rebelled in heaven and took many of the angelic host with him when he was expelled. All, including Satan, are created beings in spite of our enemy's desire to be like God. As a result, his attempts to mimic God's glory fell far short of the Creator's archetype. The resultant distortions demonstrate an absolute lack of understanding of the perfect love of God.

Satan has no authority before the throne of God, even though he is allowed access to the presence of God. He attempts to deceive even believers by means of false

---

[29] Death is not something to fear because it is at death that the believer enters into the presence of Jesus, our Lord, for eternity. In Matthew 10:28, Jesus admonishes His disciples not to fear those who can kill the body; "but rather fear him, which is able to destroy both soul and body in hell."

teachers and tactics that involve confusion and chaos. He accuses believers before God, harassing them with affliction and disease and ensnaring both the wicked and the justified with evil thoughts and deeds. Then, he tries to render us ineffective by taunting us about how terrible we are to have such wicked and sinful thoughts. As demonstrated in both the Old and New Testaments, it is only with permission from God that Satan can act against the people of God.

Other forms of satanic abuse include the prevention of God's servants from carrying out God's will and casting Christians into prison. Unbelievers remain in bondage to satanic control, but believers are free to choose righteousness in Christ. Because of the victory of Jesus Christ's redemptive death, burial, and resurrection, Christians are not subject to "possession." However, we can still be *influenced*, even oppressed, by the devil through the world and the flesh.

In spiritual warfare terms, any sinful activity that the believer does not deal with by the power of the Holy Spirit becomes a "chink in the armor" by which Satan's kingdom can gain a point of attachment and control in the believer's life. There is no acceptable compromise with sin and no room for nominal Christianity. Believers either resist the influence of the evil one who works through the flesh and the world, or they relinquish control of their lives to the power of darkness. Every Christian needs to recognize the supernatural nature of temptation and stand against it in the power of the Holy Spirit.

CHAPTER FOUR

The Loss of Innocence

The impact of spiritual warfare on humanity began with Adam and Eve. Satan enticed Eve with the same prideful desire to "be like God" that led to his own downfall.

Sin Enters the World

Satan's first angle was to plant seeds of doubt, "Did God really say … ?" He took the form of a serpent, which is described as "more crafty than any other beast of the field" (Genesis 3:1 ESV) and would have been visually familiar to Eve. That it talked to her was unusual, however. As a created being, Satan does not have the power to do the creative manipulation of nature required for such an act by the reptiles we know as serpents today. Was this a sort of satanic ventriloquism, or did God permit speech by a serpent tongue?

The sequence of events in the garden of Eden is indicative of Satan's tactics, even today:

- Humanity is deceived into mutiny, opposing God's perfect plan by a pre-existent, evil spiritual being.

- Using stealth, Satan gets the better of the hearer, in this case sinless Eve who accepts the lies and half-truths as the real truth.

- Satan is aware of the point at which her logic changes because he knows firsthand the experience of a sinless creature deciding to sin.

The consequences are always the same:

- God's creation is defiled.

- Cosmic rebellion is now an earthly rebellion.

- Humanity is now involved in the struggle and is, in fact, the focal point of the conflict.[1]

There are five long-range results of the introduction of sin into the world (the Fall):

1 **Subjective.** Instead of delighting in God's presence, man flees from God's face (Genesis 3:7–16).

2 **Objective.** God's wrath is revealed (Genesis 2:17; 3:17–19).

3 **Cosmic.** Creation is injured, and earth is in bondage to corruption, redeemable only at the "consummation of redemption" (Genesis 3:17–19; Romans 8:19–23; 2 Peter 3:13).

4 **Racial.** Sin is genetic and has been passed from

---

[1] Murphy, *Handbook for Spiritual Warfare*, 28–29.

Adam to all of mankind (Romans 5:18–19; 1 Corinthians 15:22). Deliverance can only come from God (Romans 8:18–23).

5 **Mortal.** Death, both spiritual and physical, is the universal and ultimate result of sin (Romans 5:12–14; Ephesians 2:2).[2]

The first result is subjective and leads to man's separation from God. Satan has two venues in which he is allowed by God to exert his influence. On the physical level, he is the "prince of the power of the air"; on the spiritual level, he is "the spirit that now works in the sons of disobedience" (Ephesians 2:2). The progression of man's alienation from God always leaves a vacuum which Satan's kingdom is only too glad to fill with idols (physical or spiritual) and the subsequent bondage and destruction of man. Sin, whether willful or in ignorance, opens the door to demonic influence.

In his letter to the Romans, Paul begins his arguments on this progression with the establishment of God's power and remedy for sin:

> For I am not ashamed of the gospel of Christ: for it is the power of God unto salvation to everyone that believeth; to the Jew first, and also to the Greek. For therein is the righteousness of God revealed from faith to faith: as it is written, The just shall live by faith (Romans 1:16–17).

---

[2] John Murray, "Fall, The" in Merrill C. Tenney, ed., *Zondervan Encyclopedia of the Bible* (Grand Rapids: Zondervan, 1977), #1–3, 492–494.

Paul then demonstrates that man has no excuse for denying or turning away from God because creation reveals God to mankind. Verse 19 states, "that which may be known of God is manifest in them; for God hath showed it unto them."

Romans 1:20–32 gives a detailed continuum of man's path of sin, starting with the lack of excuse for rejecting God because "the invisible things of [God] from the creation of the world are clearly seen, being understood by the things that are made, even His eternal power and godhead; so that they are without excuse" (v. 20).

Mankind "became vain in their imaginations and their foolish heart was darkened" (v. 21). They made idols of men, birds, and other creatures, changing the "glory of the incorruptible God into an image" (v. 23).

As a result, God's judgment was to give "them up unto vile affections" (v. 26), citing homosexuality specifically, and "gave them over to a reprobate mind, to do those things which are not convenient"[3] (v. 28). A list of other unrighteous acts and attitudes follows in verses 29–32. In effect, God gave Satan permission to disseminate sin (i.e., to work in the sons of disobedience because man chose to sin). Sin, then, became the consequence of sin; therefore, persistent sin is part of the punishment for sin, physical death being the penultimate result of sin. The ultimate penalty is everlasting punishment in the lake of fire alongside Satan and his servants (Revelation 20:10–15).

---

[3] The English Standard Version says, "gave them up to a debased mind to do what ought not to be done."

Seven Principles of Spiritual Warfare

Matthew 8:28–34 describes some of Jesus's miracles, which include the casting out of demons near Gadara. The account reveals seven important principles of spiritual warfare, specifically as it relates to demons.

Two men possessed with multiple demons terrorized the area so that "no man might pass by that way" (v. 28). Demonic intrusion always takes away self-control, no matter the number of demons. The demons recognized Jesus as the Son of God and, according to the account in Mark 5, even worshipped Him. They indicated that they knew His purpose on earth by asking if He was there to torment them before the time. They requested that Jesus send them into the swine feeding nearby instead of sending them into the abyss.[4]

Once they entered the pigs, they stampeded into the Sea of Galilee, killing them, and the demons were once again in a bodiless state, perhaps even driven into the fearsome "abyss." The news was spread around town. According to Luke's account, the witnesses returned to ask Jesus to leave, but at least one of the former demoniacs was found at Jesus's feet, clothed and in his right mind.

The first principle involved here is the tremendous authority Jesus exhibited by simply being able to give permission for spirits to move from humans into beasts. William MacDonald makes the point that it is strange that Jesus accedes to demonic requests. However, "If

---

[4] Notes in Thomas Nelson, Inc.'s *The King James Study Bible* for Luke 8:31 indicate "abyssos" (deep) as "the underworld, the abode of the dead (Romans 10:7), of Satan (Revelation 20:3, "pit"), and here of imprisoned demons."

Jesus had simply cast them out of the maniacs, the demons would have been a menace to the other people of the area. By allowing them to go into the swine, He prevented their entering men and women and confined their destructive power to animals."[5]

Second, Jesus is recognized by the demons as the very Son of God who has the authority to crush them. From a demonic perspective, Satan devised the death of Jesus (John 13:2, 27). When the Lord outwitted the enemy by rising from the dead and ascending into heaven, it became apparent that He had, in fact, defeated Satan and his hoards.

During the episode of the Gadarene demoniacs, however, the demons still demonstrated the defiance and disrespect prompted by ignorance. They did not have pre-knowledge of how it would be accomplished but knew they would eventually be sent into the abyss, the place where demons are imprisoned. They were already judged but not yet penalized. The military term "Legion" they gave for their name fits well with the warfare aspect of the scene.

Third, demons (even Satan himself) cannot inhabit more than one person at a time, though there is some experiential evidence of more than one "point of attachment" at a time.[6] Having been created as angels and

---

[5] William MacDonald, *Believers Bible Commentary New Testament* (Wichita, KS: A & O Press, 1989), 49.

[6] Dr. Stieglitz expressed this view during a telephone conversation with me on September 9, 2013. From experience, he described a "self-splitting" capability of demons in which points of attachment are established in more than one human. The demons are, evidently, capable of "tumbling" from one point of attachment to another at will.

able to travel within the spiritual realm at incomprehensible speeds, they are not omnipresent.[7] However, more than one demon can inhabit a body at a time. A Roman legion is between 4,200 and 6,000 soldiers.[8] There had to have been at least 2,000[9] demons to cause that many pigs to race to the water and be drowned.

Fourth, demons long for corporeal existence. They feared expulsion into the abyss. We are not told whether they went to the abyss once the swine were dead or if they were allowed to remain disembodied spirits in the region. However, William MacDonald points out, "the purpose of demons is without exception to destroy."[10] Since Jesus had initially sent the demons into swine instead of leaving them to harass people, it follows that they would not have been left to their own destructive devices upon drowning their hosts.

Fifth, demons have names and individual natures that represent their destructive purpose. The demons here collectively called themselves "Legion," but their destructive actions towards the men they possessed included a variety of anti-social behaviors: nakedness, living in the tombs, violence, accosting all who came near with brutal strength, cutting themselves with stones, and goading them into the wilderness. Though

---

[7] Daniel 10:13 describes the anonymous angel that came in response to his plea. The angel was detained for 21 days by the Prince of the kingdom of Persia until Michael came to help. Neither the angel, nor the Archangel, nor the demon charged with control of Persia was able to be in more than one place at a time.

[8] W. E. Vine, *An Expository Dictionary of New Testament Word* (Lynchburg, VA: Old Time Gospel Hour, 1952), 659.

[9] The Mark 5 account of this event records that there were 2,000 pigs in the herd.

[10] MacDonald, *Believers Bible Commentary New Testament*, 49.

not explicitly stated, despair could be added to the list since at least one of the demoniacs happily broadcast his deliverance.[11]

Sixth, Jesus values human life above that of animals, a value not shared by a world under the dominion of Satan. The accounts of this story, found in Mark 5 and Luke 8, tell us that the people were very afraid. That there were swine in the country signifies the *possibility* of sin by renegade Jews living in the predominantly Gentile region. Under Mosaic Law, it was unlawful for Jews to raise swine because they were unclean.[12] Whether they were Jews or not,[13] the herdsmen and their neighbors dreaded economic loss and begged Jesus to leave the area. Jesus demonstrated His concern for the people by causing the swine to be afflicted instead of the people. But the love of money impeded their recognition of His regard for their spiritual welfare.

The seventh principle is that all who follow Jesus are commanded to participate in sharing "what great things God hath done unto [them]"[14] (Luke 8:39). The post-demonic men were clothed, in their right minds, and at

---

[11] "He began to publish in Decapolis how great things Jesus had done for him" in Mark 5:20.

[12] *The King James Study Bible,* 1429.

[13] Jesus told His disciples not to go into Gentile areas (Matthew 10:15). When Jesus had momentous contact with Gentiles or "unacceptable" people, it is noted in Scripture (i.e., the Samaritan woman in John 4, and the Greek woman in Mark 7). In the story of the Gaderenes, however, the issue of Jew or Gentile is not mentioned. That Jesus sat down with the delivered men and no one criticized Him for it is, I believe, evidence the men were Jews in a place where many Jews lived.

[14] The command to universal evangelization in the name "of the Father, the Son, and the Holy Ghost" by Jesus's disciples is supported by Matthew 28:18–20.

least one of them was eager to travel with Jesus. But he was told to go back to his own people and share with them what God had done in his own life. No longer in bondage to satanic forces, former demoniacs are free to serve the living Christ and are equipped to take the godly stance and exercise the gifts of the Spirit in spiritual warfare. They are told to begin at home, following the sequence of evangelism found in Acts 1:8.

The World, the Flesh, and the Devil

Under the authority of Satan, the devil, there are four classifications of demons apparent from the biblical record.

1 Those free to carry out Satan's evil purposes dwell in the spiritual realm and are active on earth, afflicting and indwelling humans (Matthew 12:43–45; Ephesians 3:10; 6:12).

2 Rebellious angels are now bound in the "bottomless pit," where Satan and the currently unrestrained demons will be bound during the Millennium. Rebellious angels will someday be released once again to inflict torment on Earth for a short time (Revelation 9:2–12; 20:1).

3 Wicked angels are so evil or are guilty of such heinous crimes as to never be allowed to exist in either the spiritual realm or on earth. These are bound in "everlasting chains under darkness" and will never be released (2 Peter 2:4; Jude 6).

4 Those fallen angels who seem to be bound on earth are attached at specific geographic locations[15] (Revelation 9:13–21).

Evil spirits and demons are rebellious angels whom believers will judge (Job 4:8; Isaiah 24:21–22; 1 Corinthians 6:3). Since God's angels are "holy angels," they will not need to be judged (Mark 8:38).

For the Christian, the Bible talks of doing battle with the world, the flesh, and the devil. It is a "multidimensional sin war"[16] having to do with sanctification, not with salvation (James 4:4; 1 Peter 5:8; 1 John 3:8).

- Sin is personal—it comes from within, thus warfare with the flesh.

- Sin is social—it comes from without, thus warfare with the world.

- Sin is supernatural—it comes from above, thus warfare with evil supernaturalism (the devil).[17]

The flesh and the world are the usual channels of Satan's seduction of mankind, including believers. Even so, each of us is responsible for the choices we make regarding sin. God made us in His image, and that has not changed, even though we are sinners by heredity. Therefore, we also have the authority and the ability to resist the incursion of evil if we recognize the source of the coercion for the evil it is.

---

[15] Murphy, *Handbook for Spiritual Warfare*, 22.
[16] Murphy, Ibid., 99.
[17] Murphy, Ibid., 100.

Ray Stedman's understanding of the relationship between the world, the flesh, and the devil takes the idea of interaction a step further: "We often hear the idea, 'The enemies of the Christian are the world, the flesh, and the devil,' as though these were three equally powerful enemies. But there are not three. There is only one enemy, the devil, as Paul brings out in Ephesians 6. But the channels of his indirect approach to men are through the world and the flesh."[18]

Ephesians 6:12 tells us, "For we wrestle not against flesh and blood, but against principalities, against powers, against the rulers of the darkness of this world, against spiritual wickedness in high places."

We are then called upon to take action by "arming" ourselves for this spiritual battle. The armor can only come from God—truth around the waist, righteousness around the breast, the preparation of the gospel of peace on the feet, the shield of faith in front, and the helmet of salvation on the head.[19] Dr. Stieglitz calls these "weapons of resistance," and his list includes Truth, Righteousness, the Gospel of Peace, Salvation, Faith, the Word of God, Prayer, and Alertness.[20] All of

---

[18] Ray Stedman, *Spiritual Warfare* (Portland, OR: Multnomah, 1975), 47. Used by permission.

[19] The spiritual armor described in Ephesians 6 is explored further in chapters 5 and 6. I chose to use Spurgeon's description of the pieces from the metaphor. For a more complete discussion of the armor, see chapter 14 in Jim Logan's *Reclaiming Surrendered Ground* (Chicago: Moody Publishers, 1995), 177–186. Used by permission.

[20] Stieglitz, *Breaking Satanic Bondage*, 229. Dr. Stieglitz adds "Alertness" to the Armor of God list in his study guide *Weapons of Righteousness: Building Strong Christians for the Battle—The Three Enemies and the Four Weapons Study Guide* (Roseville, CA: Principles to Live By, 2014), 27. Used by permission.

these have their basis in serving God wholeheartedly. Nothing but the power of God can protect us from the attacks of the enemy.

Jim Logan describes spiritual warfare as the battle for the mind.[21] In his book *This Present Darkness,* Frank Peretti presents vivid word pictures of demons sitting on his characters' shoulders with their fingers in their victims' heads, stirring thoughts around. Based on my own experiences, I believe this is an apt visual portrayal of what it feels like to encounter the suggestive demonic input referred to by Mr. Logan.

Psalm 64:2–6 may also describe the nature of enemy attacks if you consider the context of this passage to refer to either human enemies or demonic enemies because of the reference to "the secret counsel of the wicked" and "the insurrection of the workers of iniquity":

> Hide me from the secret counsel of the wicked; from the insurrection of the workers of iniquity: who whet their tongue like a sword, and bend their bows to shoot their arrows, even bitter words: that they may shoot in secret at the perfect: suddenly do they shoot at him, and fear not.
>
> They encourage themselves in an evil matter: they commune of laying snares [privately]; they say, 'Who shall see them?'
>
> They search out iniquities; they accomplish a diligent search: both the inward thought of every one of them, and the heart, is deep.

---

[21] Logan, *Reclaiming Surrendered Ground,* 187.

Ephesians 6:16 makes the same kind of projectile analogy to the attacks of the wicked one as "fiery darts." Believing demonic lies, Christians sometimes feel abandoned by God when they are under attack. They choose the sin of unbelief by not trusting the promises so plainly set forth in Scripture.

One of those promises in Romans 8:37–39 clearly states that there is nothing that can separate us from the love of God. As Christians, we have the hope of God's promises in all aspects of spiritual warfare because "greater is He that is in you, than he that is in the world" (1 John 4:4). Another promise is expressed in Psalm 64 as the psalmist continues to describe God's reaction to attacks on His children, "But God shall shoot at them with an arrow; suddenly they shall be wounded. So they shall make their own tongue to fall upon themselves: all that see them shall flee away" (Psalm 64:7–8). The passage ends with human fear generated by the sight of God's actions and increased faith on the part of believers (verses 9–10).

Yet we still wonder why Satan is allowed to continue to attack the children of God and why so many Christians falter in faith when Satan is allowed to attack. In actuality, Satan is not yet allowed to do his worst. Second Thessalonians 2:6–7 describes the restraint currently being exerted in the world by the Holy Spirit. Once the Holy Spirit is taken out of the world, evil will have its way, still with God's permission. Strong delusion allowed by God to those who are unbelievers will open the world of lost mankind to belief in a lie and subsequent damnation.

Dr. Stieglitz suggests that Satan and his demons are merely following the rules God set forth when sin and corruption first entered the world. This is exhibited in the physical world when food is left to rot, or an animal dies. Maggots, beetles, and other parasitic scavengers show up to physically break down and consume dead flesh. So, too, wherever there is spiritual corruption, the devil and his demons flock to the moral decay as "God's garbage collectors," the spiritual equivalent of physical scavengers. Under God's rules, this is their function in the *kosmos*. As such, the demons need no permission to consume unrighteousness.

On the other hand, we know from Scripture that Satan cannot impact a *righteous* Christian without permission from God. Both Peter and Job were living godly lives uncorrupted by sin when Satan approached God about them. Their righteousness is why Satan had to ask permission to harass them.

Satan is not God's enemy—he knows God could crush him easily. But he is the enemy of humans. We are God's special creation, the focus of His eternal love and care. Satan seeks to attack God through human failure.[22] When the Christian engages in sin, he invites demonic attack because the sin in a Christian's life is just

---

[22] Dr. Stieglitz expressed these views during a telephone conversation with me on September 9, 2013. The construct of demons as the agents of moral decay is also explained in *Breaking Satanic Bondage*, 31–33.

as corruptive as that in an unsaved person's life. Further-more, the joy of our relationship with God can only be restored through confession and repentance.

God has promised never to leave nor forsake us (Hebrews 13:5). Likewise, He has promised to give us "all things that pertain unto life and godliness, through the knowledge of Him that hath called us to glory and virtue: whereby are given unto us exceeding great and precious promises: that by these ye might be partakers of the divine nature, having escaped the corruption that is in the world through lust" (2 Peter 1:3–4).

Summary

When Adam sinned, he gave away the authority God had granted him to rule the earth and broke the fellow-ship man had with God. In His redemptive act of death, burial, and resurrection on the cross, Jesus defeated Satan so that God could again have the fellowship and companionship of man.

Satan still remains the enemy—the father of lies, deceiver, and destroyer—with his demons to carry out his efforts to undermine that relationship at every turn. The enemy uses subtlety, complacency, and outright dis-obedience among the children of God in his attempts to annihilate God's perfect work. While Satan is allowed by God's permission to deal with Christians, God uses every attack to bring glory to Himself, having promised that nothing can separate His own children from the love of God. Those who deny Christ belong to Satan already and are part of his kingdom bound for hell (1 John 5:10–12).

While permission is required for Satan to touch God's righteous people, evil does not need permission to feed on unrighteousness. The incessant campaign against God's people requires both individual and corporate vigilance in order for believers to stand undaunted against it.

CHAPTER FIVE

God's Provision for Victory in Warfare

In *Spiritual Warfare in a Believer's Life,* Charles Spurgeon examined the story of Job with the conclusion that Satan is powerless to harm the righteous without God's permission unless, as discussed in chapter 4, there is sin in a believer's life. Both Job and Peter are examples of righteous people who were "put through the sieve," as it were, with God's permission.[1]

God Uses Even Satan to Accomplish His Will

In Luke 22, Jesus describes His Kingdom in contrasting terms to the kingdoms of the world and then tells Peter that Satan had asked to "sift you as wheat" (v. 31). He reassuringly adds, "But I have prayed for thee, that thy faith fail not; and when thou art converted, strengthen thy brethren" (v. 32).

---

[1] Charles Spurgeon, Robert Hall ed., *Spiritual Warfare in a Believer's Life* (Lynnwood, WA: Emerald Books, 1993), 57–68. Used by permission.

Here is an example of God's use of Satan to accomplish divine purposes. The outcome would clearly be to God's glory in that the event would make Peter stronger than he had been before and able to strengthen other believers. Since the conversation between God and Satan about Peter is not recorded, we don't know who started it, God or Satan. However, we do know that God started the conversation about Job (Job 1–2). As seen in the book of Job, Satan considers God's people in the following ways:

- He looks on with astonishment at the believers' faithfulness to God and His truth.

- He seeks to find a shortcoming with which to console himself.

- He sees believers as obstacles to his own agenda.

- He looks for ways to ruin them with sin to make them unfit for God's purposes.

- He looks for individual weaknesses, states of mind, and attitudes with which to undermine the believers' sense of security in Christ.

- He examines the believers' relationships, objects of affection, and conditions in the world to discover the slightest breach through which to injure us.[2]

In turn, God considers:

- How far He will allow Satan to go.

[2] Spurgeon, Ibid., 60–63.

- How He would uphold His children for the duration of the ordeal.

- How He would keep His servants blameless.

Job earned a better reward through his trial. In fact, the story of his patience and worship in the midst of incredible hardship has brought comfort and instruction to millions of Christians since. At the same time, Satan's work has been thoroughly discredited as a result of it.

Using the everyday analogy of pottery from Scripture, Spurgeon said of Job's trials, "Had the vessel not been burned in the furnace, the bright colors had not been so fixed and abiding."[3]

Jim Logan described the circumstances surrounding Job's trials in the following terms, "God did not remove His hedge of protection from around Job. He allowed Satan to fire his flaming missiles at Job and his family, to be sure. And those missiles hit home with destructive force. But the early chapters of Job illustrate a crucial principle of spiritual warfare that we all need to grasp as believers: When the flaming missiles of Satan pass through God's hedge of protection, they cease to be Satan's destructive missiles and become, instead, the refining fire of God."[4] Mr. Logan further pointed out that Job gave no credit to the devil but worshiped God instead, saying, "The LORD gave, and the LORD hath taken away; blessed be the name of the LORD" (Job 1:21).

---

[3] Spurgeon, Ibid., 116.
[4] Logan, *Reclaiming Surrendered Ground*, 123.

Like Logan, Spurgeon referred to the analogy of spiritual hostility as having the opposite effect by becoming a tool in God's hand. Using the analogy of a gardener's work, Spurgeon cited Satan's attempt to deface the tree with the ax as rendering him a pruning tool in God's hands to cut off the unproductive parts and to enhance the health and fruitfulness of the tree (i.e., the Christian). Satan's attempt to uproot the tree by digging around the roots only serves to aerate them so they can grow deeper and more solidly stabilize the tree. God's answer to satanic interference in the believer's life is to acquire wisdom and the weapons of spiritual warfare through the Scriptures so we will be strong in the Lord and know how to resist the attacks of our enemy.

David reminds us in Psalm 119:9, "Wherewithal shall a young man cleanse his way? By taking heed thereto according to thy Word."

Christ modeled the way to fight Satan when He said, "It is written" (i.e., the sword of the Spirit we are instructed to use in Ephesians 6) during His encounter with Satan in the desert. The event quickly followed Jesus's baptism, which was "the visible demonstration of Jesus's anointing for service as God's Son ... as though the voice from hell would immediately challenge the voice from heaven."[5] Linked with the work of the Holy Spirit in the Savior's life, it demonstrates Jesus's absolute submission to the will of the Father. It also demonstrates

---

[5] Williams, *The Holy Spirit, Lord and Life-Giver* (Neptune: Loiseaux Brothers, 1980), 58.

that Jesus was fully Man, subject to and enabled by the Holy Spirit to accomplish His work on earth.

In the same way, in order to individually stand firm in the victory obtained on the cross, we are to be "filled with the Spirit" (Ephesians 5:18) and the knowledge of Scripture that comes from persistent study (2 Timothy 2:15), following our Lord's example of conformity to the leading of the Holy Spirit.

Satan's Tactics of Hindrance

First Peter 5:8–9 adjures us to be sober and vigilant because Satan's activities are incessant. He is like a roaring lion, seeking whom he may devour next. We are to "resist, steadfast in the faith" and in dependence on the Lord, knowing that we are not the only ones victimized by the enemy. William MacDonald made the point that "sometimes he comes like a snake, seeking to lure people into moral corruption. Sometimes he disguises himself as an angel of light, attempting to deceive people in the spiritual realm. Here, as a roaring lion, he is bent on terrorizing God's people through persecution."[6]

Though not omnipresent like God, Satan is still found wherever one goes, aided by his fellow fallen angels. Though he persistently attempts to dissuade our walk with God using tailor-made distractions, God sees to it that our "inclinations and opportunities"[7] do not meet.

---

[6] MacDonald, *Believers Bible Commentary* New Testament, 1097.
[7] Spurgeon, *Spiritual Warfare in a Believer's Life,* 102.

Satan acts as a fowler, sneaking up on his prey to lure him into the trap. He appears as an angel of light to deceive both Christians and non-Christians alike into false doctrine and error. His attempts to consume Christians by persecution have many different faces, all devilish tactics to separate weak Christians from their convictions. Strong, persistent temptation and blasphemous thoughts insinuated into Christian minds are other ways that Satan devours. His goal is to strip us of our armor, but believers need to stand firm against the wiles of the devil because God stands with us in the battle. Our Lord and Savior has already won the victory over Satan on the cross.

In 1 Thessalonians 2:18, Paul, Silas, and Timothy were hindered by Satan from visiting the church at Thessalonica, not for lack of desiring it, and clearly not prevented by any divine intervention. The adversary attempts to undermine the believer's character before God, as seen when he tries to slander Job before the congregation of God's angels. He actively opposes the freedom of God's people and presents counterfeit versions of God's work, as when the Egyptian magicians replicated Moses's signs in order to prevent Pharaoh's decision to free Israel.

He impedes those who are new to Christ or weak believers, causing them to trip and fall over newly laid or already unstable biblical foundations by bringing to remembrance sins that have already been forgiven. He blocks Christians who are in sincere prayer when prompted by the Spirit to do any work for God, when planning or doing the work of the Lord, and when seeking to unite with one another.

Historically speaking, whenever spiritual revival has begun with the movement of strong, devoted people of God, Satan has sent counterparts to obstruct God's work by producing misleading versions of the same work. Spurgeon cites Luther versus Ignatius Loyola, Latimer and Wycliffe versus Gardiner and Bonner, as well as Whitefield and Wesley versus various trouble-makers bent on deterring them.[8]

According to Spurgeon, Satan's hindrance is detected in the following ways:

- The goal is to keep us from doing what glorifies God.

- The use of motivation that does not honor God clearly points to the evil source of the hindrance.

- What Satan puts in our way to distract us will be attractive and appealing to our human nature.

- The timing of interference is a sure sign of the origin, for instance, the thoughts that persist in diverting your attention from worship and prayer.[9]

[8] Spurgeon, Ibid., 120–121.
[9] Spurgeon, Ibid., 121–123.

The Logistics of Spiritual Attack

The subtle nature and malicious devices of the devil make not only biblical wisdom necessary but also absolute faith in the work of the Holy Spirit to withstand his attacks. Satan generally finds his victim's weakest point, his besetting sin, in order to trip the unwary. The weapons he uses against us are also tailor-made—remembered sins, past unbelief, perversions of Scripture ("it is written"). The agents he uses can be our best friends or not. The Bible demonstrates this concept with Adam's Eve, Samson's Delilah, and Solomon's many wives.

The times of Satan's attacks are also carefully chosen—during illness and grief, he tempts us to despair; he tempts us to pride at other times. He also withdraws at convenient times when he sees us spiritually slumbering, to leave us in the doldrums, so to speak.

For this reason, Spurgeon made this personal comment: "I would be afraid to exchange my temptations with another man."[10] God has given each of us faith and strength to withstand the snares He permits Satan to administer for our particular situation, not for what others are tempted to do. Stepping outside God's providence into another man's shoes might remove us from God's established protection and preparation for our particular temptations because we would then be outside the will of God. God's promises are clear: "My grace is sufficient for thee" (2 Corinthians 12:9), and "There

---

[10] Spurgeon, Ibid., 87.

hath no temptation taken you but such as is common to man: but God is faithful, who will not suffer you to be tempted above that ye are able; but will with the temptation also make a way to escape, that ye may be able to bear it" (1 Corinthians 10:13).

We are covered and protected as long as we remain in submission to God's will, according to His Word. But when we choose to allow sin to place us outside of God's will and divert us from serving Him, we step into enemy territory and open ourselves up to the scavenger aspect of demonic activity that always surrounds sin. As Jim Logan wrote, "When we are out of God's will, Satan doesn't need permission to attack us. But when we are walking in obedience and victory, we know that God has power and is protecting and refining us during tough times. Satan cannot lay a finger on us unless God allows it."[11]

The Victorious Christian Life

In his second epistle, Peter tells Christians both how to live victoriously and why we do not live victorious lives, even though Satan was defeated once and for all at the cross:

> As His divine power hath given unto us all things that pertain unto life and godliness, through the knowledge of Him that hath called us to glory and virtue: whereby are

[11] Logan, *Reclaiming Surrendered Ground,* 124.

given unto us exceeding great and precious promises: that by these ye might be partakers of the divine nature, having escaped the corruption that is in the world through lust. And beside this, giving all diligence, add to your faith virtue; and to virtue knowledge; and to knowledge temperance; and to temperance patience, and to patience godliness; and to godliness brotherly kindness, and to brotherly kindness charity. For if these things be in you, and abound, they make you that ye shall neither be barren nor unfruitful in the knowledge of our Lord Jesus Christ. But he that lacketh these things is blind, and cannot see afar off, and hath forgotten that he was purged from his old sins. (2 Peter 1:3–9)

That cleansing came when our Lord Jesus Christ fulfilled the redemptive plan of God on the cross. Jesus entered the realm of time as a man to be the Deliverer, born of a virgin. Finally, from the garden of Gethsemane to the cross of Calvary, Jesus endured a bitter battle with Satan.

Seemingly knocked out at first, Jesus pleaded that the cup of redemptive sacrifice He knew was before Him would be accomplished in another way. "Made strong by heaven,"[12] He ultimately triumphed in giving His life and then in taking it up again after three days. Chains were broken, prison doors breached, and all who believe now have access to heaven.

---

[12] Spurgeon, *Spiritual Warfare in a Believer's Life*, 17.

Then came the spoils.

Colossians 2:15 says, "And having spoiled principalities and powers, He [Christ] made a show of them
openly, triumphing over them in it." "Dividing the
spoil" is an indicator that the battle was completely won.
Satan and his servants, Death and Sin, were disarmed
and broken.

Spurgeon described the triumphal procession in
terms of Roman victors. A herald proclaiming the victo-
ries of the army precedes the procession. The pageantry
continues, led by the conquering general, the kings of
his conquest chained to his chariot. The loot taken in
battle, other prisoners, conquered flags, and the rest of
the victorious army follow.

The metaphor of the victorious Christ has His herald,
John the Baptist, leading the procession, with the Old
Testament saints following after. The serpent, writhing
and miserable, is shown as chained to Christ's chariot
wheels, trailed by the hideous fiends from hell. After that
come the rest of the redeemed, witnesses, and preachers
of the Gospel in the triumphal celebration that will continue until the last of His redeemed enter the pearly
gates. When the trumpet sounds one last time, He will
make the final ascent to heaven with His redeemed to
reign forever with God.[13]

Satan responded to the defeat with continual attempts
to destroy the work of God, harrying every step of the
believer throughout history.

---

[13] Spurgeon, Ibid., 22–27.

In the case of the demon of divination seemingly promoting the gospel in Acts 16:17, it was, in fact, a mockery and imitation of the work of God.[14] Having no other model to follow, Satan mimics the gifts and works of the Holy Spirit with counterfeits, including the gift of discerning of spirits, for his own purposes. However, the attempted duplications fall short because they are from the imagination of a created being, not from the hand of the Creator.

Satan would not attempt to stop a believer unless he or she was on the right track regarding God. Therefore, be encouraged that God has already overcome the enemy when Jesus Christ died, was buried, and rose again to redeem us from the bondage of Satan's dominion. Besides the presence of God strengthening us, vigilance and resistance with the skilled use of the God-given weapons of warfare are God's provision for victory in spiritual warfare. Ephesians 6 instructs us to put on the *whole* armor of God, "weapons of resistance"—Truth, Righteousness, the Gospel of Peace, Salvation, Faith, the Word of God, Prayer, and Alertness. And by faith, we need to make sure there are no breaches for the fiery darts of the enemy to pierce.

---

[14] *The King James Study Bible* (p. 1699) has this note for verse 17: "The strange words of the demon-possessed girl, that Paul is proclaiming the way of salvation, reveal Satan's insidious attack upon the work of God. His method is to counterfeit that which is genuine, thereby confusing and corrupting it."

Summary

Evidence for the need to be battle-ready is established by the presence of the list of armor components in Ephesians 6 and repeated biblical instructions to holiness. As Christians, we are covered and protected as long as we remain in submission to God's will; but when we step into sin, we open ourselves to predatory spiritual attack, including deceit, persecution, temptation, and blasphemous thoughts.

Warnings specific to spiritual warfare recur throughout the New Testament for the believer to be on guard and watch (1 Peter 5:6–11). The weapons God has given us for spiritual warfare are Truth, Righteousness, the Gospel of Peace, Salvation, Faith, the Word of God, Prayer, and Alertness. All of these have their basis in serving God wholeheartedly. Nothing but the power of God can protect us from the attacks of the enemy.

CHAPTER SIX

The Biblical Metaphor of the Armor of God

Wherefore take unto you the whole armor of God, that ye may be able to withstand in the evil day, and having done all, to stand. Stand therefore, having your loins girt about with truth, and having on the breastplate of righteousness; and your feet shod with the preparation of the gospel of peace; above all, taking the shield of faith, wherewith ye shall be able to quench all the fiery darts of the wicked. And take the helmet of salvation, and the sword of the Spirit, which is the Word of God: praying always with all prayer and supplication in the Spirit, and watching thereunto with all perseverance and supplication for all saints. (Ephesians 6:13–18)

It is God's Word, the Holy Bible, which establishes the metaphor of warfare in spiritual conflict. The God-given defenses provided for in the Bible reveal the thoroughness with which the Christian is equipped for this combat. Under the heading of "The Bible's Prescription for Power," Merrill Unger outlines what is necessary for Christians to "appropriate the resources at their disposal as members of Christ."[1] We must:

- Have a firm knowledge of our position and possessions in Christ.

- Have faith to act upon our position and to claim our possessions.

- Yield to God's will and be obedient to God's Word.

- Exercise prevailing prayer.

The list of armor in Ephesians 6 is a metaphorical directive that encompasses all four points in Unger's prescription. The list includes:

- Belt of Truth

- Breastplate of Righteousness

- Feet Shod with the Preparation of the Gospel of Peace

- Helmet of Salvation

- Shield of Faith

- Sword of the Spirit—the Word of God

---

[1] Unger, *The Baptism & Gifts of the Holy Spirit,* 163–172.

- Prayer
- Alertness

Preparation for Spiritual Warfare

The Bible is "the sword of the Spirit, the Word of God" of Ephesians 6:17. All of the other weapons in the list are developed in the thorough study of and application of the Word. Said to be hard to understand by those who are not believers, comprehension of fundamental and necessary concepts of the Bible is given by the Holy Spirit to those who are believers, saved by God's grace and mercy.

While Satan manipulates the Word of God when he uses "it is written" against believers, our Lord Jesus Christ did not stray from absolute biblical truth in his counterattack in Matthew 4. He *could* have chosen to exercise His Deity with divine or angelic power, blind Satan by showing His glory, or use rhetoric and logic. Instead, Jesus chose the sword of the Spirit, the Word of God,[2] as His weapon against the tempter.

It is important that this weapon, like the swords of old, be carefully sharpened by memorization and meditation so it is available for God's use in us. Mature Christian discernment and the other weapons of spiritual warfare can only come from reading, memorization, and prayerful meditation of the Bible. How will

---

[2] At the time of Jesus's "temptation" in Matthew 4, the biblical references were from the Torah, the basis of our Old Testament, and written in Hebrew.

we recognize counterfeit manipulation of the message if we do not know the true Word of God ourselves? How will we contain and resist the fiery darts of the evil one if we have chinks in our armor because we do not know the Word of God by heart? How will we remain in the center of God's peace and protection in the heat of battle if our knowledge of biblical precepts and God's promises are faulty?

Jesus used this weapon at the beginning of His ministry on earth in private when no one was near and under the most trying of circumstances. He had just fasted for forty days and nights in the wilderness. When Satan began his attack, Jesus defended His Sonship and defeated temptation with the memorized Word of God. The circumstances surrounding Him did not guide Him to do what He did; the Word was His direction from the Father. He also maintained His own spirit with the Word, remaining calm throughout the test. He handled the Word with deepest reverence, prior preparation, and thorough understanding. He stood firmly on its promises and was directed by the Holy Spirit in its use.

In spite of Satan's ever-shifting attack, Jesus continued to employ the sword of the Spirit until Satan gave up and departed. Angels were then sent to minister to our Lord. The lesson for us here is to stand against Satan with the sword of the Spirit, the Word of God. To do that requires much prayer, practice, study, and meditation on the Word, hiding it in our hearts so it will inform our thoughts, speech, and behavior and be readily usable when needed. We are exhorted to search the Scriptures diligently (2 Timothy 2:15). The Bible is not merely a historical document, but it is the entirely inspired Word of God.

Martin Luther maintained that temptation is part of our growing and learning to serve God, along with prayer and meditation.[3] The act of resisting temptation draws us into a closer dependence on God, gives us practice in recognizing the presence of God, and develops more skill in handling the armor and resistance weapons.

Spurgeon comments, "God gives us liberty, not license, and while He gives protection, He will not allow presumption."[4] While God allows temptation and testing to come, we step outside His protection if we yield to it. We learn from the life of Christ that, as we conform to the image of Christ, becoming more and more like Him, we experience a proportional increase of those things He experienced—opposition, distress over sin, and joy in the consummate walk with God.

We are encouraged by Jesus's stand in the middle of temptation in that He was tempted, just as we are; yet He did not fall, or sin, but was gloriously triumphant. We overcome the adversary by fleeing temptation (1 Corinthians 6:18–19; 10:13–14; 1 Timothy 6:6–11; 2 Timothy 2:22), praying, resisting the devil (James 4:7), exercising faith in all aspects of our lives, and by putting on "the whole armor of God" (Ephesians 6:13–18).

---

[3] Spurgeon, *Spiritual Warfare in a Believer's Life*, 87.
[4] Spurgeon, Ibid., 93.

We are soldiers and cannot safely go without any part of our armor or let down our guard at any time. Spurgeon reminds us, "You are a soldier ... In the country of a malicious enemy ... who never yet made a truce ... who never can make peace with you, nor can you make peace with him."[5]

Salvation

The helmet of "the hope of salvation" (1 Thessalonians 5:8) is a weapon of our armor that covers the head, the part of you, which, if injured, has the potential to take away all other capabilities. This is the hope that is founded on the presence of the Holy Spirit in us, the assurance and security of salvation. In other words, it is a thorough understanding of our position and possessions in God through our Lord Jesus Christ. The use of this weapon of resistance is a function of the Word of God memorized and meditated upon.

The Holy Spirit is the maker of the helmet because it is He who brings us to salvation. Salvation, represented by the helmet, renders its wearer invulnerable through truth and faith. Just as salvation gives the complete covering of Christ's protection, nothing can separate us from Him. For armies of old, the helmet was generally considered a place of honor, where the soldier's crest, plume, and other encouraging and identifying symbols could be visible to those who followed. Any other helmet

---

[5] Spurgeon, Ibid., 128.

than that of the Hope of Salvation would prove to be fatally flawed at worst and a satanic hindrance at best.

Attacks to the head include "temptations of Satan, self, and fame … from skepticism … personal unbelief … threatenings from the world … errors of the times."[6] These attacks are all equally important to avoid and are all explicitly dealt with in Scripture. "Errors of the times," however, may not be immediately recognizable from the descriptions of the church periods in Revelation 2 and 3. The times change constantly, and the errors espoused by churches in this epoch take a different form than those some 2,000 years ago.

There are four distinct types of activities that are currently "errors of the times":

- Distortion of the biblical message—the trend of using a variety of Bible translations to manipulate and distort the message.

- Syncretic worship practices—the addition of syncretic practices in church culture; in other words, the combining of different, often contradictory beliefs while blending practices of various belief systems.

- Alliance with apostate churches—the attempt to engage in combined events with other religions in the name of "unity."

- Public acceptance of beliefs and personnel that

---

[6] Spurgeon, Ibid., 130–131.

clearly contrast with biblical directives on church leadership and governance.

These all require the functioning of both the spiritual gifts of discernment of false teachings or prophecies and the discerning of spirits to determine a course of action.

The first error of the times is the trend of using a variety of Bible translations and paraphrased editions to manipulate and distort the message to match a particular agenda in both writing and preaching. This is a practice that was not widely used among evangelical Christians before the twentieth century. Because there are now so many Bible translations available, however, a historically unprecedented technique of Bible study involving the comparison of terms and interpretations in the various versions has become prevalent among both writers and preachers of the Word. If the technique is not Spirit-directed, I believe this can easily become a tool of false teaching. Too frequently, personal agendas are promoted through the manipulation of meaning and syntax in order to establish what may or may not be a biblical principle.

Even as early as his encounter with Eve, Satan tried to change the Word of God so that the message would not fully and accurately represent God to the world. In Genesis 3:4, he disputes God's Word, claiming that Adam and Eve would not die if they ate the fruit of the tree of the knowledge of good and evil.

The second error of the times is the addition of such

activities as Eastern meditative practices (Yoga, for example), circle of life models and activities (directly from New Age, Buddhist, and Hindu worship practices), prayer labyrinths, use of objects or charms for worship enhancement, visualization techniques, "Positive Thinking" procedures, and worship performance models in Christian applications. These are cited as "Satan's greatest tools of deception" by Caryl Matrisciana[7] They eventually "undermine Christian confidence in Jesus Christ as God," replacing faith in God with "faith in faith."[8] These counterfeit practices are examples of the subtlety of Satan in diverting Christians from biblical application to unwittingly worship false gods within the very sanctuaries built in Jesus's name. The addition of Christian phrases, for instance, as mantras for meditative chanting and physical positions advocated in Eastern religions do not change the function of worshipping the false gods to whom they were meant to appeal.

A third error of the times is the attempt of modern churches ("emergent") to "put aside differences" in the name of "tolerance" and "unity," both ignoring biblical injunctions to holiness within church leadership and teaming up with other religions in ecumenical settings. The use of alternative worship practices, as described above, is only one of the fusion possibilities. Second Corinthians 6:14 makes the biblical exhortation to separation from such practices clear: "Be not unequally yoked

---

[7] Caryl Matrisciana, *Out of India* (Menifee, CA: Caryl Productions, 2008), 178.
[8] Matrisciana, Ibid., 171.

together with unbelievers: for what fellowship hath righteousness with unrighteousness? And what communion hath light with darkness?"

As an example, the preaching and worship practices of an Islamic Imam or a Jewish Rabbi who rejects Jesus as Messiah are not in any way compatible with those of a born-again Christian. According to a recent visitor to Israel, some Christian Jews he met wondered at Western Christians who tour Israel and then attempt to emulate the practices of Judaism, putting themselves back into bondage to the law from which they were saved.

For the same reasons, Christian churches need to be very careful about aligning with other religions and cults who use a biblical vocabulary but whose bases of belief are in different gods. These religions deny Jesus as the incarnate deity, and their salvation is founded on individual works instead of Christ's redemptive act on the cross. Since these concepts are diametrically opposed to biblical Christianity, there is no common ground for agreement.

In recent years, many high-profile Christian leaders have compromised and desecrated both their message and their churches through "multi-faith" events. In order for ecumenism to work and unity to be kept in such a situation, biblical principles have to be surrendered—a satanic strategy to render us ineffectual in proclaiming the Gospel of Jesus Christ to the world.

The fourth error of the times involves embracing

within church membership, even leadership, people whose very salvation is biblically questionable. The trend towards acceptance of homosexual pastors, approval of same-sex weddings, and other "woke" distortions, for instance, clearly condones lifestyle sin that the first epistle of John condemns as indicative of unbelief. Too many churches have split and been destroyed by the incorporation of culturally-compelled tolerance of long-term sin, which is contrary to biblical truth. We live in an age of gross negligence of biblical truth in many churches that leave congregations without a moral compass of godly leadership.

The "Helmet of Salvation" is necessary to avoid these snares. Since we accepted Jesus as Lord and Savior by faith, the Holy Spirit has resided in us. Each person within the body of Christ receives gifts of the Holy Spirit and exercises them with increasing effectiveness as they mature spiritually. Our common salvation places us in relationship with one another, whereby we use our gifts to the benefit of the whole body of Christ and for the glory of God. Ideally, our knowledge of scriptural promises related to our hope in Christ and the benefits of our position in Him support the tasks necessary to protect the body of Christ from these errors of the times.

Because of the blatant nature of Satan's attacks on Christians in general and the church specifically, those gifted as discerners of spirits are especially needed in churches today. To step back in ignorance and let the subtlety of Satan infiltrate our churches in these ways and with incompatible beliefs and practices, denies the holiness and righteousness God requires His people to guard and brings into question our own salvation.

The Gospel of Peace

The feet shod with the preparation of the Gospel of Peace are of divine construction, paid for by the enormous price of the shed blood of Jesus Christ. They provide perfect peace with God, a delight in His will, and conformity to His Word. Peace toward ourselves and others is inherent in the wearing of these shoes because our Lord Jesus Himself displayed peace in the middle of difficult circumstances throughout His life. The shoes fit perfectly, give their wearer a firm foothold in truth, and are entirely suitable in that "a sense of pardoned sin and reconciliation with God fits us for anything and everything."[9]

They effectively preserve the wearer's feet and are good for both climbing and fighting. Just as Jesus trampled the serpent underfoot,[10] we can overcome the snares of Satan because of our understanding of our position and the subsequent claim by faith to the resources of that position in Christ. This is why we as Christians can obediently rejoice and trust the conditional promise of peace that passes understanding given in Philippians 4:4–7.

---

[9] Spurgeon, *Spiritual Warfare in a Believer's Life*, 147.
[10] Psalm 91 prophetically describes Christ. Verse 13 says, "The young lion and the dragon shalt thou trample under feet." In addition, Genesis 3:15 describes one of the consequences of the fall as the woman's seed ("it" singular) shall bruise Satan's head.

The Shield of Faith

The "Shield of Faith" is necessary because the fact of our salvation and the peace of God within us do not spare us the blows of Satan. When the blows come, faith protects the armor and the believer against attack by receiving the blows that are meant for him. To do so, like a shield, it must be strong, of heaven's forging, and a single piece with no seam. Unless one's faith rests on truth alone and is entirely aligned with the Word of God, the "shield of faith" will not completely protect. There will be chinks through which the fiery darts of the enemy can penetrate. The ability to remember the promises of God and to understand the doctrines of salvation and Scripture enables the Christian to handle the shield of faith with skill based on cumulative experiences with faith.

The metaphorical shield is not only for protection, but it is also an emblem of honor carrying the warrior's coat of arms, in this case, the cross of our Lord Jesus Christ. We identify our faith with the cross because the Bible tells us, "I am crucified with Christ: nevertheless I live; yet not I, but Christ liveth in me: and the life which I now live in the flesh I live by the faith of the Son of God, who loved me, and gave Himself for me" (Galatians 2:20).

While the helmet and shoes can stop only those darts aimed at them, the shield of faith stops all the darts hurled by the enemy. The Ephesians 6 reference to the whole armor of God uses the words "above all" in connection with the shield of faith, placing a greater importance and emphasis on faith than on any other part of the armor. Since the use of all of the metaphorical pieces of the armor requires faith, the shield is the centerpiece of the metaphor and all other parts depend on faith to function properly.

The Sword of the Spirit

The "Sword of the Spirit" is the final metaphor of the believer's occupation with spiritual warfare and the only part of the armor that is offensive as well as defensive. The Sword of the Spirit is the Word of God which, when wielded under the direction of the Holy Spirit, can either bring what is hidden to light or cause grievous wounds "to the dividing asunder of soul and spirit, and of the joints and marrow" (Hebrews 4:12).

The Word is God-breathed, inspired by God. Not only was the Word inspired in its writing but it is still inspired as the Holy Spirit continues to move the hearts of humans through Scripture. Without the presence of the Holy Spirit, the "sword" would have no edge. It is only through the Holy Spirit that believers can stand, resist, and fight in this spiritual warfare.

The sword is necessary for the Christian's battle. The war is very real and persistent. We are told to take up the sword and "we are not told that we may lay it down."[11] The mandates of God's people are to stand fast and win souls. God has fitted us with all we need to carry out His will.

---

[11] Spurgeon, Ibid., 173.

To illustrate some of his points, Spurgeon includes references to John Bunyan's allegorical *Pilgrim's Progress.* He cites Christian passing through the valley of the shadow of death to demonstrate the roaring of Satan in blasphemies whispered in the ears of God's people.[12] Describing Satan's subtlety in his "withdrawings," Spurgeon refers to Bunyan's Enchanted Ground where the devil did not go because the people were asleep. There was no need to disturb them when they were deceived into lethargy already. Satan did his work with Christian in the Valley of Humiliation.[13] The scene in which Christiana and Mercy faced the big dog and fiery darts of the enemy is referred to in connection with the shield of faith. No matter what Satan brings against you, "know that there is nothing that can bring joy and peace into your heart but faith."[14]

The Bible makes it very clear that God is still sovereign even in the face of the severest of spiritual battles. God allows and uses for His own purposes everything the enemy throws at us.[15] We are purified by the battles, humbled, and brought to a deeper dependence on our Lord and Savior. Without this testing, our faith would not grow. God has made redemptive provision for His own, and He continues to build His Bride, those who are born again by faith into His Church, to be God's Royal Consort, to reign with Him in the future (2 Tim-

---

[12] Spurgeon, Ibid., 161.
[13] Spurgeon, Ibid., 36.
[14] Spurgeon, Ibid., 161.
[15] See chapter 5 for clarification on the analogy of Satan's attacks as tools in God's hands.

othy 2:12). He will exert judgment and final exile from His presence of the Evil One once all the prophecies are fulfilled—and no one knows when that will be, not even the incarnate Jesus[16] (Acts 1:7; 1 Thessalonians 5:1–3).

"We glory in tribulations also: knowing that tribulation worketh patience; and patience, experience; and experience, hope: and hope maketh not ashamed; because the love of God is shed abroad in our hearts by the Holy Ghost which is given unto us" (Romans 5:3–5). Until that day comes, we are called to "Rejoice evermore. Pray without ceasing. In everything give thanks: for this is the will of God in Christ Jesus concerning you. Quench not the Spirit. Despise not prophesyings. Prove all things; hold fast that which is good. Abstain from all appearance of evil" (1 Thessalonians 5:16–22).

Summary

While the allegory of war is alluded to throughout Scripture, the metaphor of Roman armor demonstrates most graphically the thoroughness with which Christians are equipped by God to do spiritual battle. At the same time, God is sovereign and uses the bellicose attempts of the enemy to purify, humble, and bring us to a deeper dependence on our Lord and Savior. As discerners, we

---

[16] Revelation 20 describes Satan's judgment. First, he will spend the millennium of Christ's reign on earth, bound with chains in the bottomless pit. Then he will be released to deceive the nations for a short time, only to be thrown into the lake of fire and brimstone to be tormented day and night forever and ever along with all of his followers. For at the judgment, at the great white throne, "whosoever was not found written in the book of life was cast into the lake of fire" (Revelation 20:15).

must not flounder because of lack of faith. Scripture makes it clear that by the grace of God, we have been given everything we need for life and godliness (1 Peter 1:2–3). In addition, Luke 10:19–20 reminds us that Jesus said, "Behold, I give unto you power … over all the power of the enemy: and nothing shall by any means hurt you. Notwithstanding in this rejoice not, that the spirits are subject unto you; but rather rejoice, because your names are written in Heaven."

CHAPTER SEVEN

My Pursuit of Insight

One of the objectives of this book is to help others understand what the gift of discerning of spirits looks like in personal development and practical application. Let me share with you how I identified the God-given gift of perceiving spiritual warfare activities and how I moved forward in maturing in that gift. No one will have the same experience or sequence of events as I did. However, by viewing my own unfolding of comprehension, you may be able to recognize common threads of development in your own gift of discerning of spirits.

Discerning of Spirits Gifting Discovery Sequence

My parents had very recently become Christians at the time I was born. Throughout my childhood they were wholly devoted to learning scriptural truths and sharing these with their young family. Furthermore, we were part of a church where the teaching was well-grounded in biblical truth and solid spiritual formation. Having come to know the Lord Jesus as my Savior while still a child, I grew up with extensive Bible teaching, which included instruction on the gifts of the Holy Spirit.

During my teen years, I sensed a spiritual "cocoon" of sorts protecting me. I pursued an understanding of what my spiritual giftedness entailed, and I found that I was led towards encouragement, prayer, and ministry (called "helps" in the list of gifts found in 1 Corinthians 12:28). With maturity came a lessening of the isolation and protection I had perceived earlier in my life, as well as occasional onslaughts of the sensation of evil in certain places and circumstances that I had not recognized before. Because I did not understand, I fled, more often than not, from the situation that caused such discomfort.

It wasn't until I was in my late twenties that I finally began to understand that I was discerning spiritual warfare. As a wife and mother, I still confused the experiences with the cyclic, emotional activity related to physical changes brought on by pregnancies and the challenges of dealing with three small children.

Repeatedly, I called upon the Lord to remove the affliction that caused me to feel what I interpreted as depression. Even though there may have been some physically-induced bouts of emotional distress, I began to recognize a pattern. I was most profoundly affected during meetings at church, quite often even at the point of entering the church building. I presumed it was a spiritual attack that Satan was using to dissuade me from attending church. Though I believe that is a valid assumption and probably true in part, additional observation clarified what God was indeed asking of me through all of this.

I began to realize that I was generally excited to be going to church when Sunday or midweek meetings rolled around. In spite of the occasional recalcitrant child and accidents that are always possible when getting children ready to go somewhere, I would get to church ready to worship and enjoy the fellowship. But once there, I would find myself deeply disturbed to the point of wanting to flee the scene. Sometimes, these feelings occurred as I walked into the building. At other times, it would happen after I had been sitting in the sanctuary for a while.

After much prayer, the Lord finally revealed the pattern to me, which was related to the presence of another believer in the congregation. Over subsequent weeks, I could see that any time I experienced a spiritual struggle upon entering, she was in the building already.

Conversely, if she wasn't there, I didn't experience the agitation until she arrived. As a result, God prompted me to begin praying for her. It was as if I was experiencing her emotions vicariously. The woman cited has not been the only person in whom I recognized demonic entanglement in church. Each time it occurs, I am prompted to pray.

This discovery has evolved into "praying the perimeter."[1] Even before I walk through the doors of the church, I am lifting the building and the congregation up to the Lord, verbally denouncing the enemy and his cohorts in Jesus's name and by His shed blood. As the meeting proceeds, there are times when I recognize a breach in the hedge of protection for whatever reason, and God lets me understand exactly how to pray that breach back into His protection.

The Expansion of Active Perception

I continued to learn about spiritual warfare, and I have learned to recognize other settings in which I have discerned spiritual battles raging. For example, one time, my family and I looked for a place to have dinner before attending a concert in another city. We chose a franchise sandwich shop for our meal. As we entered, I was stopped at the door as if by a physical hand on my chest. The feeling of an evil spiritual presence was overwhelming. I'm sure the proprietor and the only other customer there were completely confused when I turned to my family and said, "We're not supposed to be here. We're supposed to be at the one at the other end of town."

The other shop of the same franchise was next to a park and across from the church where the concert was to be held. While my family ate dinner at that park, my husband had the opportunity to share the gospel with a

---

[1] The concept of "praying the perimeter" is discussed at length in chapter 10, "Specialized Prayer Forms in Spiritual Warfare."

man nearby. God's hand was definitely in that experience, and He was glorified by it.

More recently, I found myself feeling nauseated for no visible reason as I approached the cashier in a local store. There was a young man checking out in front of me. I looked at him and saw that he was heavily tattooed and pierced. His face was veiled in darkness so that I could not make out his features. This was not the first time I have been unable to see the face of a person who is demon-possessed. As soon as he walked away, the nausea disappeared. Years ago, I would have remained bewildered by experiences such as this. Now I recognize it as a reaction to the presence of demons.

At other times, God has revealed the "faces" of evil to me. The first time I realized this was happening, I was again in a fast-food restaurant. When I entered the building, my first thought was, "These are the ugliest people I have ever seen." It was disturbing to look at the faces of the workers because they appeared to be photographic double images, like a special effect in a movie. I recognized the presence of the spiritual "cocoon" even though I could see visible representations of spiritual beings attached to these people. When I shared this experience with Dr. Stieglitz, he said it wasn't unusual for people with the gift of discerning of spirits to actually see demons attached to people.

God's Protection

The "cocoon" is a gift from God, a kind of spiritual covering for my protection that surrounds me whenever I exercise the gift of discerning of spirits. Frequently, there are times when I feel overwhelmed with the spiritual input from demonic activity around me. God has been gracious to shield me at those times so that I can focus on prayer specific to the situation. I especially needed it when I finally recognized that there was a demonic stronghold in our house that sometimes sent me reeling with terror from our bedroom. I was able to rid the house and property of that stronghold by verbal confrontational prayer or "power prayer," a concept discussed in chapters 10 and 12.

After a visit to our church some years ago, Dr. Stieglitz was having lunch with my husband and me, along with the rest of our church leadership team. I told Dr. Stieglitz of recent events in my life that pointed to a definite spiritual gift of discerning of spirits and asked him for a list of books that might help me sort through what I was experiencing. After asking me some key questions, he turned to our pastor, who was also present at the meal, and told him that his church was very fortunate to have a "gatekeeper" in its midst to keep the church protected by specific prayers related to the spiritual battle surrounding the congregational meetings of the church and other ecclesiastical functions.

Since then, God has continued to lead me through a maturing of the gift. At first, I could not find any books written on the subject of discerning of spirits by which other believers with this spiritual gift may be encouraged.[2] That is why, based on my study of the Bible, books about spiritual warfare that Dr. Stieglitz had recommended, other pertinent books from my own Bible study library, and my experiences with discernment as a "gatekeeper" for my church, I believe God led me to publish what I have learned about the gift of discerning of spirits.

What I experience is indeed bizarre to those who have never encountered it and who do not have the same gift. There are some Christians who would say that these incidents do not come from God but from Satan. For example, Mark Bubeck states, "For too long the work of demons has been dismissed by most of us as a curious, vaguely understood phenomenon in animistic, heathen cultures, but it was not considered a problem which might invade our lives, our homes, our churches."[3] He continues to describe the American Christian as apprehensive regarding spiritual warfare in general: "To openly challenge intruding demons, as did our Lord and the early disciples, was considered dangerous and far too extreme by mainstream evangelicals. To hear of a missionary casting out demons sent chills of fear through

---

[2] Note: Since *The Gift of Seeing Angels and Demons: A Handbook for Discerners of Spirits* was first published in 2017, several other authors have also published books on the subject.

[3] Bubeck, *The Adversary,* 17. Used by permission.

most American Christians, who secretly thanked God that demon-possessed people were not in America."[4]

However, the world's fascination with wizardry, the occult, and Eastern religions, along with the increase in crime, addictive behaviors, and legislated immorality, cannot be ignored.

Demonic and Satanic efforts that were clandestine in the past have become more pervasively evident, blatant, in fact, than ever before, even in America. In today's decaying world, it is essential for more Christians gifted with discerning of spirits to recognize the underlying spiritual battles and respond to them with godly prerogative (on their knees).

With each encounter, I gained an increased understanding of these experiences. The outcome has always been prayer, counseling, exhortation, and/or recognition of the need for help. Because God is the center of my response, and He is glorified by the outcome, I know that this is a spiritual gift from God.[5]

Summary

As one who is gifted with discerning of spirits, God led me to a marginal comprehension of this gift by revealing the patterns of experience and the corresponding events.

---

[4] Bubeck, Ibid., 17.

[5] William MacDonald, *Believers Bible Commentary New Testament*, 1133, 1135–36. First John 3:7–8, 23–24, and 4:1–6 make it clear that actions that are righteous represent the presence of the Spirit of God. Without the instigation and direction of the Spirit of God, the actions emanating from the discerning of spirits would not be of God.

When I asked Dr. Stieglitz about relevant reading material, he cited books on spiritual warfare. But neither of us found anything written specifically on this aspect of discerning of spirits.

In the face of increasing demonic activity in the world, God is equipping His people to stand in the face of the enemy, some through discerning of spirits. Through my own experience of finding nothing previously published about discerning of spirits, God prompted me to write on the subject, only one step in His preparation for the increased need of those gifted in discerning of spirits. The validity of the gift is demonstrated by the God-honoring outcomes.

CHAPTER EIGHT

Determining Your Giftedness

Do you think God might have granted you the spiritual gift of discerning of spirits? This is the ability to see, sense, smell, or perceive the presence of angels and demons, as well as the activity connected with their presence. Merrill Unger says that the implication of a gift of the Spirit is a continuous ability to exercise the gift effectively and repeatedly.[1] The ongoing demonstration of the ability to recognize spiritual activity, both inside and outside the church walls, is a good indicator of giftedness in discerning of spirits. Perhaps you are as confused as I was about the sometimes-bizarre feelings and experiences you have dealt with since you became a Christian.

Understand Your Holy-Spirit Gifting

Before you became a Christian, you were not gifted with any of the gifts of the Holy Spirit, and you were not

---

[1] Merrill Unger, *The Baptism & Gifts of the Holy Spirit*, 139.

able to perceive the activity of spiritual beings from a Christ-centered perspective. Once you become a Christian, however, you are given spiritual gifts by the Holy Spirit, which enable you to serve God according to His will. With the gift of discerning of spirits comes the ability to perceive, sense, and sometimes smell or see angels and demons, as well as to identify their activities.

Sorting through these disturbing encounters can be unnerving and overwhelming if you do not understand what is happening and where it is coming from. Satan would have you remain in confusion and ignorance on this effect because you are the radar of spiritual warfare, which we know is an extremely important role in the spiritual battles that rage around us. But as you grow in the Lord and become stronger in your faith, you will perceive more and understand better what it is that God requires of you in any given situation.

To determine if you have the spiritual gift of discerning of spirits, follow these steps and ask yourself these questions:

- Pray.
- Re-study your weapons.
- Look for patterns.
- What happens when the perception goes away?
- Have you ever physically seen demons or angels?
- What are the outcomes of these events?

Start by praying about it. Make sure you are studying

the Word of God, walking with the Lord according to His Word, and "confessed up" with God. The study and application of the principles in Dr. Stieglitz's book, *Spiritual Disciplines of a C.H.R.I.S.T.I.A.N.*, is a good starting point. If there is habitual sin in your life, deal with it before the Lord so you will be able to hear that still, small voice of God when it comes in answer to your prayer for clarification. James 5:16 says, "The effectual fervent prayer of a righteous man availeth much." While Christ makes us wholly righteous at the time of our salvation, Jesus pointed out to the disciples that the dust of the world needs to be frequently washed off "our feet," so to speak (John 13:6–10).

Check that your protective "armor" (i.e., the weapons of spiritual warfare as described in chapters 5 and 6) is in place. Prayerfully re-study the Scripture passages in those chapters (Ephesians 5; 6; Colossians 2:25; 1 Thessalonians 5; 1 Peter 1:3–9; 5:8–9) to ensure that you are fully under God's "umbrella" of protection and so that you will not be distracted from God's direction for you. The weapons with which we fight the enemy are Truth, Righteousness, the Gospel of Peace, Salvation, Faith, the Word of God, Prayer, and Alertness.

Look for patterns in the events surrounding your experiences of depression, sudden nausea, or intense emotional disturbance for no apparent physical or natural reason. Are they connected to the presence of particular people or when you are in particular places? "James" (not his real name) tells of being in New Orleans one time and finding himself feeling ill much of the time. He was sick to his stomach, and his hair stood up as if he were experiencing a chill. He began to pay attention to where he was and what was going on around him when he experienced these feelings. He noticed that the physical indicators would pass as he left the vicinity of certain buildings where demon-related occupations were pursued, like palm reading, tarot cards, and death-cult-oriented novelty shops.

When you detect patterns of oppression, ask God to show you who or what you need to pray for. Since all Christians are instructed to "pray without ceasing" (1 Thessalonians 5:17), this is a discipline you need to develop no matter what your gifts are. However, in all aspects of spiritual warfare, prayer coverage is especially important, whether it is acting as "radar" or participating in spiritual warfare activities such as deliverance.

Do these feelings of depression, illness, or intense disturbance stop when you are no longer in the presence of those people or in those places? As it was for James, this is a distinctive clue to your giftedness in spiritual discernment. Remember, Satan and his demons are not omnipresent, even though they are able to travel at incredible speeds. When you distance yourself from the physical site of the sensations that appear to be discerning-of-spirits-gift related, the perceptions of spiritual discomfort should dissipate. Be aware that this is not always the case, though, as I have sometimes experienced attachments that have gone with me. At those times I have called upon others to cover me in prayer in order to allow me to exercise extensive and directed power praying to get rid of them.

Have you ever "seen" or perceived the activities of demons or angels? For me, the experience of physically "seeing" demons seems as if I were looking at a photographic double exposure. A woman I interviewed says she saw a large, dark being with big triangular teeth and striated musculature crawling up the wall of her daughter's house. Another discerner of spirits saw a demon in the form of an old hag.

Not everyone with the gift of discerning of spirits "sees" demons or angels, but it is a possibility with this gift. I think Christians, who serve the same God that the angels serve, frequently see angels in human form without recognizing them. Hebrews 13:2 tells us to "Be not forgetful to entertain strangers: for thereby some have entertained angels unawares."[2]

What are the outcomes of these events? Godly responses include praise of God, prayer, godly counsel, exhortation, righteous action, or spiritual warfare. They demonstrate the God-given, God-directed, and God-glorifying nature of the gift of discerning of spirits.[3] Any other outcome renders questionable the origin of the event and the motives of the person demonstrating the gift.

---

[2] For more information see chapter 14, "Discerning Angelic Activity."
[3] These are discussed more extensively in chapter 9, "The Outcomes of Discerning of Spirits."

The outcomes of counterfeits of this gift range from merely self-serving to obviously demonic in nature. Once you have determined that you are indeed experiencing the spiritual gift of discerning of spirits, be vigilant to keep your "armor" and weapons of spiritual warfare (Truth, Righteousness, the Gospel of Peace, Salvation, Faith, the Word of God, Prayer, and Alertness) active and well-maintained through regular worship, confession, praise, prayer, Bible study, meditation, and fellowship.[4]

What to Do with This Gift?

If, after answering the questions above, you feel you have the gift of discerning of spirits, here are suggestions about what to do with this gift:

- Ask God for direction.

- Ask for God's protection.

- Find mature Christians to comprise a prayer support and accountability team.

- Report information you receive through discerning of spirits to your pastor or spiritual leader.

- Help your church leadership team to understand this gift if they do not.

- Ask God to lead you to others who understand the gift.

---

[4] For additional information see *Spiritual Disciplines of a C.H.R.I.S.T.I.A.N.*, Stieglitz, 2011.

First, ask God for direction in understanding and using this gift for His glory. Just as it is with all the gifts of the Spirit, each person gifted with discerning of spirits has a unique experience and God-directed work connected with their giftedness. I am led primarily to be a gatekeeper for my church and a prayer warrior. I am also led at times to exhortation, counseling, and power encounters in which I command evil spirits away in the name of and by the blood of Jesus Christ. Others are able to determine the names and activities of demons to facilitate the work of those involved in deliverance events. A pastor gifted in discerning of spirits can readily recognize when new "ministries" proposed to him are Holy Spirit-inspired or if they are powered by the enemy of our souls.

Second, in all "discerning of spirits" events, ask God to cover you with His hedge of protection (the "cocoon") so that you may proceed with what He calls you to do in any given situation. In keeping with the warfare metaphor, without this hedge of protection, you will find yourself distracted from the primary function of your gift. Instead of acting in the role of radar and sonar, you will end up blindly fighting the battle without radar in place.

Third, seek mature Christians with whom you can share your experiences and request to be prayer warriors and accountability partners for what you do. You may feel physically alone in your service with this gift, so your prayer team is an important part of the ministry of discerning of spirits in standing in the gap for you. I frequently ask God to prompt my prayer team to pray for me. It is important to communicate with your prayer team often, keeping them informed with the understanding of their importance to what you do. When I am able, I use an e-mail distribution list to let my team know when I need them to pray; then I follow up with as much information as I can give, depending on the nature and confidentiality of the situation.

Just as the radar operator in the military reports any suspicious activity his equipment has perceived to a section chief, you need to take the information you have received through discerning of spirits to your pastor, elder, or other spiritual leader. Your church pastor and elders may not understand your ministry in the church. But if they do, they will understand your need for covering prayer, the need of the church for the gatekeeping you do, and the value of the advanced information you can give concerning coming spiritual attacks on the body of Christ. Prayerfully help shed light on this gift for those in spiritual authority over you.

Other Christians around you may not understand your experiences. Most have never had the window into the supernatural open up to them in the way that God has given those gifted in discerning of spirits. Your experience of continual awareness of the supernatural world defines your existence in a unique way. As you grow in faith regarding this spiritual gift, ask God to lead you to those who will understand for counsel, mutual encouragement, and so forth so that you can use the gift of discerning of spirits unhindered.

God has given each of us certain gifts and they are not all the same. We are not all equipped to do the same jobs, but all the jobs are necessary for the good of the Church (1 Corinthians 12:17, 20–23). Recently, I had lunch with a friend who is preparing for a lay counseling ministry. She said that the outcome of her giftedness is in compassion and mercy. We both laughed as I proclaimed that I am so not gifted in either of those except for what we are all called as Christians to exercise in both areas. By the same token, the gift of discerning of spirits is absolutely outside of her experience and understanding as far as the gifts of the Spirit are concerned. All of the gifts are needed for the body of Christ to function as God intended.

Biblically, this concept is demonstrated in Acts 8, when Simon the sorcerer appeared to become a true believer. Philip accepted his conversion at face value, not demonstrating the gift of discerning of spirits. It appears, however, that Peter was able to recognize Simon's perfidy as the actual presence of demonic influence and satanic bondage when Simon tried to buy an apostolic position of authority.

Your Other Holy Spirit Gifts

Quite often, God gifts us with more than one gift for the working of the body of Christ. If you have never done so, you need to determine what all your spiritual gifts are. Have you ever taken a spiritual gifts survey to determine your spiritual gifts? The Principles To Live

By website (ptlb.com) has one under its "Resources" tab. Click on the heading "Discover Your Spiritual Gifts." This may help narrow down your possibilities and give you a better idea of the ministry for which God has equipped you alongside discerning of spirits.

While the Principles To Live By survey gives an adequate place for all aspects of the gift of discernment, many spiritual gift surveys and inventories will not have enough information to tell you that you have the gift of discerning of spirits. Remember, very few Christians recognize a function for discerning of spirits outside the recognition of false prophets and teachers. This includes many of the authors of spiritual gift inventories. Even so, a spiritual gift survey or inventory will help you pinpoint peripheral gifts that God has given you, refining and defining the part you play in your church as a spiritual discerner.

Summary

I have found from experience that personal discovery in maturing the gift of discerning of spirits must begin with prayer and expertise with the weapons of resistance in spiritual warfare (Truth, Righteousness, the Gospel of Peace, Salvation, Faith, the Word of God, Prayer, and Alertness). The next steps are to look for patterns of perception and the environment and associations connected to those perceptions. Then, seek God's guidance for the outcomes of those perceptions and establish a prayer and accountability support team.

Besides discerning spirits, God may have granted you other Holy Spirit gifts for the health of the body of Christ. A spiritual gift survey will help you discover what else God is directing you to accomplish within your church connection.

CHAPTER NINE

The Outcomes of "Discerning of Spirits"

Let's take a look at what is involved in discernment events to understand the outcomes and implications of discerning of spirits.

The Intrusion of the Supernatural

Earlier, I expressed the experience of discerning of spirits in metaphors related to "an open window (momentary glimpse) from the physical world into the spiritual world, or an intrusion of the supernatural into the natural world by the heavenly host." The ability to perceive the activities of the spiritual side of our world is not given to all Christians. However, I believe that God allows some of us to see through and, at times, traverse through dimensional barriers that are solidly prohibitive and opaque to those not gifted in this way (Isaiah 6:1–8).

As humans, we are each "essentially a spiritual being in the image of God [and] there is no part of life which can be rightly treated as not related to the spiritual nature or to the spirit world."[1] Since we are bound by the limitations of our physical bodies, however, it is difficult to understand the concept of experiencing the spiritual world. By God's enabling gift, the discerner of spirits is able to perceive from a dimensionally-bound existence into a reality (the spiritual world) that has no dimensional boundaries that we can comprehend. It is as if we see like the angels do, which is an amazing concept to consider, humanly speaking.

Part of the initial discomfort of this experience comes from a spiritual "lack of gravity," so to speak. It is a disturbance of our sense of being clothed in our bodies. Second Corinthians 5:1–4 expresses the innate human need to be "clothed" by a body of some kind, especially the desire to be clothed with the heavenly, eternal bodies prepared for us by God. As a result, we acutely feel the effect of the physically corrupt nature of our biological bodies when we are exposed to the spiritual world in discerning of spirit events. In other words, we sense a vulnerability to the spirit world, a sort of nakedness, when we begin to learn to practice the gift of discernment that God has given us. This is why it is so vital to ensure that we remain under the protection of God, not only during events involving the gift of discerning of spirits but also all the time. As we become more skilled in discerning of

---

[1] Warner, *Spiritual Warfare*, 43.

spirits, we more readily recognize when to seek God's protection and pray, reducing the discomfort and increasing the ability to fully and joyfully serve in this capacity.

While God has chosen to work through humans on this earth, each of us is held responsible for God's direction in our lives, exclusive of human wisdom and inspiration. As Christians, our responsibility is to fight spiritual warfare with the most effective God-given weapons backed by the power and authority of God. He has given us the authority and power to bind satanic activity and to shred demonic bonds through our direct line of communication with Him and in His name.

Ministry to the Glory of God

Scripture and experience have taught me that exercising the gift of discerning of spirits always leads to ministering to people, whether directly or indirectly. For me, the outcomes have always been prayer, godly counsel, exhortation, and/or a recognition of the need for help (i.e., righteous action or spiritual warfare).

First, the initial action should always be prayer. While exhortation and warning are possible outcomes of discerning of spirits, the initial action should not be to warn the individuals. God is the one who gives us this awareness of the spiritual realm, and He is the one who directs our actions as a result. Direct interaction with God in prayer is the first line of defense. After prayer, we are able to follow up with whatever God directs us to do, whether that action is to notify those in spiritual authority, exhortation of whoever is involved, or other actions related to spiritual warfare.

This is also true of both Old and New Testament events. Balaam's donkey gave godly counsel that led Balaam to prayer first and then action. He blessed Israel instead of giving the curse Balak had requested (Numbers 22:22–23:12). When David saw the angel, he prayed first, and then he acted in obedience to God's instructions given through Gad (2 Samuel 24:17–19). Elisha prayed that his servant would also see the God-sent army on the hills around them (2 Kings 6:13–17). Nebuchadnezzar's sighting led to the acknowledgment of the power of God and the removal of Shadrach, Meshach, and Abednego from the furnace (Daniel 3:24–30). Communication was the result of Daniel's encounter, with action taken in response to the message the angel brought to him (Daniel 6:20–23).

In the New Testament, Jesus's use of discerning of spirits in Matthew 4 led to the reproof of Satan with the two-edged sword of the Word of God (spiritual warfare). His rebuke of Peter and the deliverance of the demoniacs of Gadara were also examples of spiritual warfare.

Knowing they would be frequently engaged in spiritual warfare, Jesus gave his disciples authority over all demons (Matthew 10:1, 8; Mark 6:13). Elated that even the demons obeyed them in the name of Jesus, their faith increased so that they could go on using the gift of discerning of spirits to know what to pray for and what action to take—whether it was healing from illness or deliverance from demons. The result of Peter's encounter with Ananias and Sapphira in Acts 5:1–6 was exhortation in the form of accusation and rebuke. God's revelation of the true motivation for their deception ended their lives and, in this case, acted as an example for all who heard of it.

Just as in the Old Testament, angels and other spiritual non-demons were sometimes visible in the New Testament. Peter's sighting of the angel resulted in action—he followed the angel out of prison (Acts 12:7–10). The sight of Moses and Elijah with the transfigured Jesus on the mountain caused the disciples to make the misguided offer to build tabernacles for Jesus, Moses, and Elijah. Hearing the voice of God in the cloud led to fear, then to obedience (Matthew 17:2–9; Mark 9:3–10; Luke 9:29–36).

The Logistics of Discerning of Spirits

Concerning prayer in general, S. D. Gordon said, "You can do more than pray after you have prayed, but you cannot do more than pray until you have prayed … Prayer is striking the winning blow … service is gathering up the results."[2]

Prayer is the first response and imparts the winning blow when the gift of discerning of spirits is exercised in any given situation. Divine protection and guidance are necessary to interpret and further act on the encounter, the process of "gathering up the results."[3]

---

[2] Paul E. Billheimer, *Destined for the Throne* (Fort Washington, PA: Christian Literature Crusade, 1975), 51.

[3] Billheimer, Ibid.

Once the spiritual discerner recognizes spiritual input, the reaction needs to be the question, "Lord, what do you want me to do in this situation?" Sometimes, the input from spiritual conflict is so sudden and overwhelming it is not recognizable. Because of the enemy's lies, it is easy for the discerner of spirits to be knocked down and dissuaded from focusing directly on the episode as a spiritual conflict. For example, the day our church began to broadcast a local Christian radio station, I was there for a weekly prayer meeting. I felt agitated as soon as I walked in and found myself snapping unkindly at another person in the building. I apologized, but the damage was done.

It wasn't until I sat down in the prayer room next to the radio room that I realized the horrendous weight of spiritual warfare I was bearing. I felt ill to my stomach and wanted to flee. The attack was so strong and disturbing that I could not concentrate on prayer before I asked God to "cocoon" me so that I could focus on the battle. Once safely "inside," the sensation of His increased protection enabled me to think straight. In the name of Jesus, I verbally commanded Satan and his emissaries away from our building. This action is also known as "power prayer."

The "cocoon," what I call the perception of God's protection at such times, is a kind of spiritual sanctuary of refuge when we exercise the gift of discerning of spirits. Once the protective "cocoon" is in place, the discerner is able to concentrate on prayer for the specific battle. Being able to look on from the "other side of the mirror,"[4] so to speak, allows the discerner to be separate from the struggle and to differentiate how to pray effectively without having to fight through the battle at the same time. There are those who are so sensitive to spiritual battles that they cannot physically remain in that location; they actually have to go to a different location in order to effectively pray.

Second, those with the gift of discerning of spirits must crucify daily the old sin-trained flesh, walk in accordance with who we are in Christ, and "be transformed by the renewing of our mind" (Romans 12:2). To focus on one's own walk with God, making sure the whole armor of God is in place, and our relationship with God is without hindrance, is of primary importance. Always keep in mind that to be protected by God's armor, "We need to live in truth, we need to act righteously, we need to be peacemakers when the battle becomes intense, we need to be ready to take God-designed risks, look for God's ways of escapes, listen for God's whispers of His word to give us wisdom, cry out to God for direction, and remain alert to Satan's schemes!"[5]

It is very important to understand who we are in Christ in order to live and grow in the Christian life, especially with regard to efficiently carrying out the direction God gives us through spiritual gifting and

---

[4] This is a metaphor relating to law enforcement interrogation rooms that have a one-way mirror so that others can look on without being directly involved in the proceedings.
[5] From notes by Dr. Stieglitz. For more information on this subject, see his book, *Secrets of God's Armor.*

prayer. According to Neil Anderson, "A Christian, in terms of his or her deepest identity, is a saint, a spiritually-born child of God, a divine masterpiece, a child of light, a citizen of heaven. People cannot consistently behave in ways that are inconsistent with the way they perceive themselves. You don't change yourself by your perception. You change your perception of yourself by believing the truth."[6]

In addition, Mr. Anderson cites the requirements of the "essence of Christian maturity." "First, it requires a firm understanding of who you are in Christ. You can't become like Jesus unless you are His divine offspring. You have to be grafted into the vine because apart from "Christ you can do nothing"[7] (See John 15:5).

Third, our function as discerners of spirits requires the grace of God as is true for all God-directed activities. "For sin shall not have dominion over you: for ye are not under the law, but under grace" (Romans 6:14). We cannot live righteous lives by human effort based on external standards. Under the covenant of grace, we live by faith according to what God says is true in the power of the Holy Spirit."[8]

---

[6] Neil T. Anderson, *Victory Over the Darkness* (Ventura, CA: Regal Books, 2000), 47.
[7] Anderson, Ibid.
[8] Anderson, Ibid., 90–91.

The Nature of Intercessory Prayer in Discerning of Spirits

Since personal prayer is an essential factor of God's work in the life of every Christian, several kinds of prayer are identified in Scripture. In 1 Timothy 2:1, we are exhorted that "first of all, supplications, prayers, intercessions, and giving of thanks, be made for all men."

Here is a good outline for our everyday "prayer-closet" time with the Lord, with the addition of confession from the so-called "Lord's Prayer" in Matthew 6:9:

- Worship
- Confession
- Intercession
- Supplication
- Petition

Carl Knott and William MacDonald contend, "It is not always easy to define or distinguish [between the components of prayer]. What is important is that we storm the throne of grace in behalf of others and for our own needs."[9] MacDonald further explains, "We would not be overrating [the importance of prayer] if we say that it is the atmosphere in which the soldier must live and breathe. It is the spirit in which he must don the armor and face the foe. Prayer should be continual, not sporadic; a habit, not an isolated task."[10] According to

---

[9] Carl T. Knott, Jr. and William MacDonald, *Does It Pay To Pray?* (Scarborough, Ontario: Everyday Publications Inc., 1994), 5. Used by permission.

[10] MacDonald, *Believers Bible Commentary New Testament*, 769.

Andrew Murray, prayer has two functions in the believer's life: "one, to obtain strength and blessing of our own life; the other, the higher and the true glory of prayer, for which Christ has taken us into His fellowship and teaching, is intercession."[11]

As an outcome of a discerning-of-spirit event, prayer has qualities not necessarily found in normal Christian living and communicating with God. Worship and confession have their place in preparation to serve God with this spiritual gift. Supplication and petition generally happen as aftermath consultations and periodic "debriefings" with God, covering and repairing the damage done by the Evil One in a given spiritual warfare event. Intercession and prevailing prayer, however, are key to spiritual warfare.[12]

John G. Lake (1870–1935) was a missionary to South Africa during the early twentieth century. Because of a devastating fever epidemic in the region, a quarter of the population died over the course of a month. A native intercessor began a prayer vigil against the plague. The vigil lasted days, and Lake asked him on several occasions if he was getting through. The answer was always, "Not yet." One day, he told Lake that if he had "just a little help in faith, my spirit would go through." Lake kneeled down to join the man in prayer.

---

[11] Andrew Murray, *The Believer's School of Prayer* (Minneapolis, MN: Bethany House Publishers, 1982), 50.

[12] See Chapters 10 and 11 for more thorough information on the subject of personal prayer.

During his time in prayer, he found himself moving away from the spot and was given an occurrence of discerning of spirits so that he saw "a multitude of demons like a flock of sheep. The Spirit had come upon him [the intercessor] also and he rushed ahead of me, cursing that army of demons, and they were driven back to hell, or the place from whence they came. Beloved, the next morning when we awoke, that epidemic of fever was gone."[13]

Ezekiel 22:30 paints the picture of a military strategy—that of covering a gap in the wall in wartime, standing with weapons firing to protect the breach in the wall, thus not allowing for invasion. Ezekiel 13:5 also bemoans the lack of someone in the gap. The context of the metaphor in both verses is that of God, who is ready to destroy Israel for the false prophecies and divinations upon which the spiritual walls have been repaired. The protective walls are weakened by the sins of the prophets, and there is no one to stand and advocate for Israel in prayer. No one at the time of Ezekiel had acted with discernment to stop the false prophets and the destructive consequences of their sin. Protecting the gap in the wall continues to be a metaphor for the spiritual battle going on outside of our physical perception. Now, Jesus Christ is our advocate before God (1 John 2:1).

---

[13] Gordon Lindsay, *The New John G. Lake Sermons* (Dallas: Christ For The Nations, Inc., 1979), 29–30. Used by permission.

While discernment is a universal Christian function requiring biblical maturity, God also placed those especially gifted in discernment and discerning of spirits within our congregations for the protection of the body to stand in the gap and intercede before God, in Jesus's name, on behalf of the body of Christ. "Gatekeepers" for the church is one way Dr. Stieglitz describes this function of those who are able to detect spiritual activity.[14] As created human beings, we are bound by the dimensions of time and space. Those gifted in discerning of spirits are gifted with the ability to not only perceive the gap (in other words, the battle) beyond those dimensions but also to stand and fight that battle in prayer.

Based on the Hebrew word for intercession, paga (which means "to meet"), Dutch Sheets described intercession in terms of representing Christ on Earth. Our Lord is the intercessor as He represents us to God in Heaven. "Intercessory prayer is an extension of the ministry of Jesus through His Body, the Church, whereby we mediate between God and humanity for the purpose of reconciling the world to Him, or between Satan and humanity for the purpose of *enforcing the victory of Calvary* ... Our intercessory prayer will always and only be an extension of His intercessory work."[15]

God created man in His own likeness so that "God was recognized ... in humans."[16] Having sinned and

---

[14] Dr. Stieglitz has mentioned this concept to me in several conversations over the years.
[15] Sheets, *Intercessory Prayer*, 42–43. Italics are mine.
[16] Sheets, Ibid., 27. See also 1 Corinthians 11:7.

fallen "short of the glory of God" (Romans 3:23), "we must be changed back into God's image 'from glory to glory' (2 Corinthians 3:18) for this recognition to be realized again."[17] The Bible is very clear that our relationship to answered prayer is governed by our relationship to God.

Holy Scripture gives us assurance that "the love of God is unconditional, but His favor and blessing are not."[18] While we cannot lose our salvation once we accept Jesus Christ as our Lord and Savior by faith,[19] disobedience to God and a lack of faith can hinder our prayers from being answered. If we remove the power of God from our lives and ministry, the results are reduced effectiveness and an invitation to demonic attack.

Summary

Godly responses to discerning-of-spirit occurrences include praise of God, prayer, godly counsel, exhortation, righteous action, and spiritual warfare. Adjustment to the understanding of giftedness in discerning of spirits includes calling upon God for protection, seeking mature Christians to comprise a prayer and accountability team, reporting warnings and intelligence received through discerning of spirits to your pastor or spiritual leader, and helping your church leadership team understand this gift. In addition, ask God

[17] Sheets, Ibid., 27.
[18] Sheets, Ibid., 83.
[19] Hebrews 13:5 tells us God will never leave us nor forsake us.

to lead you to others who understand this gift and can encourage you to mature in your gift.

It is important to see prayer as the first response to spiritual warfare. There are four types of prayer in the arsenal of the discerner of spirits. The prayer for protection gives you a shield from which to observe and concentrate on praying through the battle instead of being in the thick of the battle. Personal prayer is where your daily strength is acquired from God. It includes worship, confession, intercession, supplication, and petition. Praying the perimeter and power prayer are covered in chapters 10 and 12.

CHAPTER TEN

Specialized Prayer Forms in Spiritual Warfare

First Thessalonians 5:17 tells us to "Pray without ceasing." Although ceaseless prayer is given as a general admonition to all Christians, it is especially important for discerners of spirits to be in constant communication with the source of our power. The enemy of our souls would love nothing more than to destroy that which protects and alerts church leadership to his efforts at distraction and damage.

The Power Behind Prayer

The power behind prayer is God; access to that power comes from a close walk with Him, submitting to His will, and "abiding" in Him. First John 3:22 says, "And whatsoever we ask, we receive of Him, because we keep His commandments, and do those things that are pleasing in His sight." As our walk with God matures, our ability to direct His power through prayer during spiritual warfare becomes more accurate. John Williams states, "Spiritual power in our lives is not the product or reward for our praying, searching, pleading, tarrying, or striving; but the gracious gift of our Sovereign Lord, and it is manifest when God's believing people are clean and willing."[1]

We know God by experience in ever-increasing faith, and we have been given His Word, the Bible, to communicate to us what we need for godly living. Psalm 27:14 states, "Wait on the LORD: be of good courage, and he shall strengthen thine heart: wait, I say, on the LORD."

According to Dutch Sheets, "It is the simplicity and purity of devotion to Christ that must be the springboard for everything we do."[2] Faith without works is dead; in other words, walking in the righteousness that God, in our Lord Jesus Christ, has bought for us is the only authentic outcome of our salvation (James 2:14–26). The Bible clearly tells us the parameters of the promises given to us:

- Psalm 91 tells us that we know we must dwell in the secret place with God.

- Ephesians 6:13–18 reminds us of our need to be fully armored for spiritual warfare.

- James 4:7 and 1 Peter 5:8 urge us to resist the devil.

---

[1] Williams, *The Holy Spirit, Lord and Life-Giver*, 13.
[2] Sheets, *Intercessory Prayer*, 151.

Furthermore, the Bible makes it clear that all Christians are soldiers in a war, wrestling against the powers of darkness (Ephesians 6:10–13). Besides resisting the devil, we are to exercise God-given power over him and his demons (Mark 3:14–15; Luke 9:1; Acts 1:8; Ephesians 1:8–2:10; 2 Timothy 1:7).

Murphy puts it like this: "Seated with the cosmic Christ, sharing His throne, is the cosmic Christian. As the cosmic Christ, He is Lord. He is God. As the cosmic Christian in Christ, I am a man of cosmic power. It is His power, which operates within me. As the cosmic Christ, His sphere of operations is the entire universe … His operations in the heavenlies and on earth all relate to salvation history—His love for humanity. As a cosmic Christian, my sphere of operations is the same as His, that is, in the heavenlies and on earth. I am seated with Him in the heavenlies; I am also indwelt by Him on earth … [In Ephesians 1] Paul takes the believers into the heavenlies (v. 3). He reveals that these heavenlies represent not only the sphere of their Christian life in Christ (vv. 13–18), and the locale in which Christ is enthroned as Lord, but also the locale of the activity of the powers [that are manipulating humans towards evil demonic goals] (vv. 19–23)."[3]

How else would it be possible to "overcome the world"? As 1 John 5:4–5 (ESV) states, "For everyone who has been born of God overcomes the world. And

---

[3] Murphy, *Handbook for Spiritual Warfare*, 394–395.

this is the victory that has overcome the world—our faith. Who is it that overcomes the world except the one who believes that Jesus is the Son of God?"

The Bible does not say that Jesus delivered us from Satan's power; He delivered us from Satan's authority (gr. *Exousia*), the right to use his power on us[4] (Luke 10:19; Colossians 1:13, 2:15). The legal hold Satan had over us (because Adam relinquished God-given sovereignty to him) was dissolved in Christ. We are no longer bound by Lucifer's works. We are given authority over Satan, in Jesus's name, for casting out demons, binding and loosing regarding the devil's agents, and prevailing against the gates of hell. Second Corinthians 10:3–5 reminds us of the spiritual nature of the weapons to which we have access in this war:

> For though we walk in the flesh, we do not war after the flesh: for the weapons of our warfare are not carnal, but mighty through God to the pulling down of strongholds; casting down imaginations, and every high thing that exalteth itself against the knowledge of God, and bringing into captivity every thought to the obedience of Christ.

While each instance of spiritual confrontation is dealt with differently, according to God's direction, our primary defense is intercessory prayer to bind satanic forces and, thereby, tear down strongholds through prayer.

---

[4] Sheets, *Intercessory Prayer*, 163.

Since Christ's work of intercession involves both the acts of reconciling and separating, much of our function of continuing His work of intercession also involves both. More than just asking the Father for victory, it involves wrestling and prevailing in prayer.

According to Arthur Mathews, we already have victory in Christ's redemptive death on the cross and resurrection on the third day. However, "It does need a man to lay hold of that victory and precipitate a confrontation with the enemy, and resist him."[5] Since creation, God has chosen to work through humans on Earth. Human prayer releases the answer to Christ's intercession on our behalf and the power of the Holy Spirit to accomplish it.[6]

Knott and MacDonald remind us that "the effectual fervent prayer of a righteous man availeth much" (James 5:16). "We never come closer to omnipotence than when we pray in the prevailing Name of the Lord Jesus. We will never be omnipotent, even in heaven, but in prayer we wield more power than we can ever do in any other way … It is an amazing thing that our God-given will can be used to hinder and oppose Him by our unwillingness to pray."[7]

Spurgeon said, "Prayer is the forerunner of mercy … You will find that scarcely ever did a great mercy come

---

[5] R. Arthur Mathews, *Born for Battle* (Robesonia, PA: OMF Books, 1978), 113. Used by permission.

[6] Mathews, Ibid.

[7] Knott and MacDonald, *Does it Pay to Pray?*, 27. Used by permission.

to this world unheralded by supplication ... prayer is always the preface of blessing."[8] According to R. A. Torrey, like the spiritual revival of Acts 1, all true revival since New Testament times has happened as a result of human prayer.[9]

Praying the Perimeter

Relative to discerning of spirits, quite often intercession comes in the form of praying the perimeter. For the discerner of spirits, praying the perimeter is the same as standing in the gap and acting in the capacity of church gatekeeper. The spiritual gift of discernment (against false preaching and teaching) would cover the aspect of what is *preached* within the sanctuary[10] and prayers on that behalf would also be considered a "standing-in-the-gap" measure.

The gatekeeper intercedes against all other invasions from the enemy. This person is "praying the perimeter" which is direct intervention for spiritual conflict taking place against the hedge of heavenly troops surrounding any gathering of God's people. A break in the wall of angels standing guard on the congregation might come from a demonic presence distracting part of our Royal Guard in order to breach the perimeter of protection. It could also come in the form of a demonic presence brought into the congregation by whoever it is that the

---

[8] Knott and MacDonald, Ibid., 30. Used by permission.
[9] R. A. Torrey, *How to Pray* (New Kensington, PA: Whitaker House, 1984), 97.
[10] Sanctuary here takes the broad form of anywhere that a body of believers meets to preach and hear the Word of God.

presence is attached to (or influencing), whether they are Christians or not.

As we saw above, the Bible frequently exhorts us to holiness and to don "the *whole* armor of God" (Ephesians 6:11). That we are so warned and still given specific instructions for spiritual warfare indicates that there are believers who decline to take heed, opening the gate for demonization and for carrying those attachments into the sanctuary. Praying the perimeter involves binding demonic presence within the sanctuary.

Power Encounter

Spiritual warfare prayer on the part of one gifted in discerning of spirits also involves binding the enemy with direct, confrontational language commanding Satan and his emissaries to leave the site, an action called "power prayer."[11] It is a direct confrontational intervention in the name of and by the blood of Jesus. This is one way to "resist the devil, and he will flee from you" (James 4:7). It is used in the context of corporate worship as well as in any spiritual warfare involving the body or the physical structure of the church. This is the kind of prayer I used, as related above when I sensed the tremendous burden of spiritual warfare in our church building the morning the radio station housed there began broadcasting.

---

[11] The first time I heard this designation was after a pre-service prayer meeting. I sensed a great deal of spiritual activity in the place where we were to meet and I used direct, confrontational language to break the stronghold of demonic presence there. A pastor approached me and asked if I was the one who had used the "power prayer." When I said that I was the one, he nodded thoughtfully and walked away without any other comment.

This kind of power praying (using direct, confrontational language) is not just for spiritually gifted gatekeepers. Neil Anderson relates the story of a young woman named Daisy, a Christian who began to manifest serious mental and emotional problems after her parents divorced. She complained of snakes crawling on her at night when she was in bed. Her antidote was to run to her mother. But the snakes came back when she was alone. Neil told her, "When you are in bed and the snakes come, say out loud, 'In the name of Christ I command you to leave me.'" She denied that she was mature enough, and he reminded her that it is not a matter of maturity; it is a matter of our position in Christ. "You have as much right to resist Satan and make him leave as I do."[12] Daisy came back a week later with the news that the snakes were gone.[13]

While these events don't necessarily reflect the kind of discerning that happens for a church gatekeeper, they do bring into focus the common element of crossover from the spiritual realms to the physical that prompts a gatekeeper to action. God allows us to recognize evil spirits at work, even to the point that we are able to see them, hear them, and smell them.

---

[12] Neil Anderson, *The Bondage Breaker* (Eugene, OR: Harvest House Publishers, 1993), 57.

[13] Anderson, *The Bondage Breaker*, 58. Neil Anderson continues that Daisy was free of demonic entanglements within a few months. "If her problems had been strictly neurological or caused by chemical imbalance, taking authority over the snakes in Jesus's name would not have worked." In Daisy's case, the problem was spiritual, and "five years of hospitalization and chemical treatments hadn't worked."

Edward Murphy relates an event in his life that happened when he decided to live entirely for God and become a missionary. As a result of his newfound faith, his Catholic mother had disowned him and his fiancée had broken the engagement. A Catholic priest had told him that if he left the Catholic Church to become a Protestant missionary, he was doomed to hell.

One morning, he awoke to find an evil presence in his room that used the priest's words, all lies, to undermine Ed's assurance of salvation. Praying, attempts to resist, and using God's Word as a sword were ineffectual and did not dissipate the utter panic of this attack that continued for a week, leaving him too ill to get out of bed. Finally, Ed was able to pull himself to a prayer meeting of his fellow students, where he found release and peace through praying God's promises of life and peace in His Son. As he continued to pray for some days after, he gradually found complete release from the attack and restoration to the joy of his salvation.[14]

In this kind of audible refutation of demonic attack, using the Word of God is not unusual in spiritual warfare. That it took some time indicates that the prayers instigated a battle. As with Daniel, in Daniel 2, the ongoing release of power to heavenly warriors resulting from prayer ensured the battle was won. For Ed, the answer for which Jesus had already interceded was released.

---

[14] Murphy, *Handbook for Spiritual Warfare*, 90.

Murphy's experience falls under the category of a "power encounter." Murphy defines a "power encounter" as "a crisis point of encounter in the ongoing spiritual warfare between supernatural personages in which Christians are directly involved. Its goals are the glory of God, the defeat of the 'no-gods' (Galatians 4:8–9), and the obedience of men to the one true God and His only begotten Son."[15]

As with biblical accounts of spiritual discerning, each modern power encounter, whether dealing with deliverance issues or praying the perimeter in a congregation, is different in detail and magnitude. Each must be dealt with according to the direction of the Holy Spirit. However, whether it is by praying God's promises back to Him with the use of Bible verses in prayer, binding the enemy, breaking down strongholds, or resisting the devil by using direct, confrontational language, as believers, we know that we have the *authority* to overcome Satan and his demons. *God has promised this in His Word.*

The Bible speaks to all Christians in James 4:7: "Resist the devil, and he will flee from you." Neil Anderson reminds us that "if you don't resist him, he doesn't have to go … Resisting the devil in your life is your responsibility based on the authority you have in Christ."[16]

While we have been delivered from the authority of Satan, we have not been delivered from the presence of Satan. He is a liar and a thief, and he will keep us

---

[15] Murphy, Ibid., 540.
[16] Anderson, *The Bondage Breaker*, 58.

in bondage through deception, stealing the peace of God through ignorance of our status with God. Furthermore, he will enter the sanctuary with us to obstruct worship and the preaching of God's Word in any way he can. That's where the gatekeeper is so necessary to God's assembled congregations.

Precepts of Spiritual Warfare

Based on Scripture, this is what spiritual warfare is about. While it may seem odd to those not gifted in this way, the recognition of this is a common experience to those of us who are enabled to exercise the gift of discerning of spirits. Think in terms of the spiritual "sightings" from both the Old and New Testaments, as surveyed in chapter 2. Think of Ezekiel 1 and the imagery of the living creatures with wheels within wheels. Then think of Revelation and the armies coming from heaven to fight in the physical world.

Though there is some biblical information that describes the spiritual realm, much of it is difficult for humans to comprehend. This is the result of limitations in both human language and human boundaries within physical space. Paul explained, "Now we see through a glass darkly; but then face to face: now I know in part; but then shall I know even as also I am known" (1 Corinthians 13:12).

C. S. Lewis described the physical plane as the "shadowlands," in contrast to the spiritual world, the "real" world in his perception.[17] His *Screwtape Letters*, populated with a hierarchy of demons bent on destroying God's work on earth, is another apt representation of spiritual warfare from the demon's point of view.[18]

What happens in the spiritual plane of existence has direct application to the physical world. This direct correlation of the physical world to the underlying and incessant spiritual battle is implicit throughout the Bible. For example, in spiritual realms, there seems to be a tangible factor to words, which are abstract concepts in the physical world. Jesus is called "the Word" in John 1, and by "the Word," all things were made. In the physical world, spoken words by themselves cannot, by any stretch of the imagination, create something tangible.

Discerning spiritual conflict is the recognition of warfare happening in that other "plane" of existence, the spiritual realm. It is not possible for that awareness to occur without intervention from the Holy Spirit and the results of that awareness are also directed by the Holy Spirit.

---

[17] C. S. Lewis, *The Last Battle* (New York: Macmillan, 1970), 169–170, 183. In *The Last Battle*, the final book of *The Chronicles of Narnia Series*, Lewis presented the idea of "shadowlands." "The Narnia you were thinking of ... was not the real Narnia ... It was only a shadow or copy of the real Narnia ... just as our own world, England and all, is only a shadow or copy of something in Aslan's real world ... as different as a real thing is from a shadow or as a waking life is from a dream." Aslan tells the children that they are "in the Shadowlands—dead ... The dream is ended: this is the morning." Lewis further explores this idea in *The Great Divorce*.

[18] Lewis, *Screwtape Letters*, 103–107.

Depending on the situation, there are other outcomes to exercising the gift of discerning of spirits after the initial response of prayer. Sometimes godly counsel is called for. During a service one time, I was led to privately pray about the marriage relationship of an acquaintance in specific terms that God had revealed to me. The woman approached me after the service *without knowing of my prayers for her* and asked to talk. She shared her burden, and I was able to direct her to Scripture with godly counsel and to pray with her.

Discerning of spirit prayers are generally not heard by other people. While "power prayers" are either whispered or uttered out loud, prayers for protection, personal prayer, and perimeter praying occur in the quietness of the heart as church services proceed.

Led by the Holy Spirit, there are times that I am also called to speak a word of exhortation to specific people for whom the Lord has directed me to pray. One Sunday, a young couple I had never met before came into a church service. Having recognized demonic entanglements entering with them, I was directed to pray for them. The Lord did not reveal the details as He sometimes does (another aspect of the gift of discerning of spirits).

During our conversation after the service, it came out that they were Christians, but they had chosen to live together in sin, not being married. As a result of what I had perceived and by the prompting of the Holy Spirit, I was led to remind them that their cohabitation was not in keeping with obedience to Christ. I was a little hesitant because I was new to understanding the gift of discerning of spirits. God used this instance to strengthen my understanding of the gift and my faith in His leading as a result of the gift. Even though I had never met these people, they thanked me and accepted the words I quoted from Scripture. I continued to pray for them during the week. They returned the following Sunday, having decided to marry instead of continuing to live in sin.

Finally, recognizing the need for help is also an outcome. My husband and I were asked to attend a prayer meeting of elders to specifically address a family's concern for their daughter's health. She had been ill off and on for a long time, losing weight and having no strength. After many tests, the doctors were not able to come up with a diagnosis. As part of the service, the girl was anointed with oil. During prayer, I became aware of a demonic presence in the room. The Lord revealed to me the demonic entanglement with the girl. Immediately, I was led to power pray, leaving several other prayer warriors gasping. Aside from the pastor, the people in the group had never experienced direct, confrontational intervention in prayer before. Lacking a biblical understanding of spiritual warfare, the parents were offended that I would suggest any such attachment.

The family refused to deal further with the issue as a matter of spiritual warfare. The girl seemed better for a week and then became ill again. The family moved away soon after, and I do not know the outcome of the girl's illness. However, from this experience, I learned to prepare people who have never experienced power prayer. I find I need to speak of what I am about to do, explain why I am about to do it, and how the prayer will be spoken. There was also no follow-up on the spiritual warfare issues from my church leadership team because none of them understood it themselves.

Because the gatekeeper's work in discerning spiritual conflict is related to the local church, the leadership, whether it is a pastor-led or elder-led church, needs to be informed. They need direct communication so they can do their job of shepherding and follow-up on spiritual warfare issues like that cited above. Besides teaching those with the spiritual gift of discerning of spirits, the purpose of this book is also to enlighten church leadership personnel about the tremendous prayer and ministry resource a discerner of spirits can be for both their ministry and their congregation.

The gift of discerning of spirits can also play a vital role in power encounters with the purpose of permanent release (deliverance) from demonic oppression and possession. Dr. Stieglitz writes, "When the gift is refined and developed, there is the ability to know the name, work, and attachment of a demonic spirit … One woman I have worked with had the gift of the discernment of spirits. She had developed this gift to a high degree. On one occasion, when she did not accompany the deliverance team, I called her on the phone to ask the name of the demon and its work. She prayed and gave me a name and an activity. I went back to the session armed with her information and made substantial progress in the session."[19]

One of the people Dr. Stieglitz has called when he is involved in intense spiritual warfare says that the information does not come all at once. In her experience, she can only ask one question about demonic identity and nature at a time and write it down. Until she writes it down, God does not allow her to continue. But when she gets through the questions in this manner, she is able to give the information Dr. Stieglitz needs for spiritual warfare to continue. Another contributor who has aided Dr. Stieglitz in the same way says that he merely prays, and the information comes to him.

While the experience of the God-given gift of discerning of spirits is unique for each person so gifted, the outcomes are always God-directed and God-glorifying. For me, the outcomes include prayer, godly counsel, exhortation, and/or a recognition of the need for help. The prayer outcomes have included power praying, praying the perimeter, or intercession. That is not to say that these are the only outcomes of the gift of discerning of spirits in other Christians.

Summary

God is the power behind all prayer. Our ability to tap into that power requires our obedient walk and constant communication with the Lord. We are called to

---

[19] Stieglitz, *Breaking Satanic Bondage: Intensive Training In Spiritual Warfare*, 48–49.

both resist the devil, wrestle and prevail in prayer, and rout him from strongholds by the power of Jesus's name. Besides prayer for protection and personal prayer, the discerner of spirits also uses perimeter prayer and power prayer.

Praying the perimeter is used in an assembly of believers and involves standing in the gap in intercession for those present, binding the enemy, and upholding the royal heavenly guard that is there for the protection of God's own people. Power prayer is the direct, confrontational commanding away of evil spirits, backed by the authority of God, in the name of and by the blood of our Lord Jesus Christ. In each instance of spiritual warfare, the discerner of spirits must follow the leading of the Holy Spirit for direction after prayer.

CHAPTER ELEVEN

About Personal Prayer

When we talk about personal prayer for the discerner of spirits, we are talking generally about prayer for all Christians. First Thessalonians 5:17 adjures us to "Pray without ceasing." The primary occupation of our risen Lord is ceaseless prayer as He intercedes for us (Hebrews 7:25– 28). Fellowship with our Lord Jesus Christ is seriously compromised when we don't spend time in prayer.

Dual Purpose

Personal prayer is both a weapon of warfare and a matter of spiritual health in our relationship with God. All that we do as discerners of spirits and as warriors in spiritual warfare is based on our spiritual health. In John 15:4, Jesus said, "Abide in me, and I in you. As the branch cannot bear fruit of itself, except it abide in the vine; no more can ye, except ye abide in me."

To abide in Christ means to be unconditionally dependent on Him. We cannot expect to hear from God and exercise our God-given spiritual gift, no matter what the gift is, if we do not spend personal time with our Lord and Master. Time alone with God—being still to wait on Him (Psalm 46:10), reading and meditating on His Word, cleansing our walk with confession, and presenting our concerns in prayer to Him—is crucial to having victory both in our personal lives and in our work of standing in the gap. We cannot stand in the gap when we have gaps in our own lives.

George Mueller (1805–1898) was a man known for his faith in God. He relied entirely on answered prayer for God's provision in his life. His faith in God was demonstrated by the administration and funding of orphanages that ultimately fed, clothed, and housed thousands of homeless children based solely on donations. He read the Word of God on his knees as part of his worship and prayer time. His biographer, Arthur T. Pierson, commends the value of this habit in terms of four principles:

- This habit is a constant reminder and recognition of the need for spiritual teaching in order to [understand] the Holy Oracles. Pierson further cites the renewed reverence for the Scriptures and dependence on their Author for insight into their mysteries.

- Such a habit naturally leads to self-searching and comparison of the actual life with the example and pattern shown in the Word of God, [leading one naturally to confession].

- The words thus reverently read will be translated into the life and mold the character into the image of God.

- The Holy Scriptures will thus suggest the very words which become the dialect of prayer.[1]

When we pray like this, we have no need to ask whether we are praying in the will of God or not; being molded to the image of God through the Word and accompanying prayer brings our thoughts and prayers into alignment with the will and character of God. By the same token, negligence or distraction regarding meditation on God's Word destroys our ability to pray in harmony with the Holy Spirit.

Regarding personal prayer, Knott and MacDonald identify five categories of prayer, adding confession to the 1 Timothy 2:1 list:

- Worship is what the disciples did as Christ ascended, leaving them in Bethany with the promise of spiritual enabling to carry out His final instructions found in Luke 24:50–53.

- Confession is necessary to "abide in Christ," as John 15:7 states. In the so-called "Lord's Prayer," Jesus Himself told the disciples to ask for forgiveness (Matthew 6:9).

- Intercession is described in Ezekiel 22:30–31.

---

[1] Arthur T. Pierson, *George Muller of Bristol: His Life of Prayer and Faith* (Grand Rapids: Kregel Publications, 1999), 139–140.

When we intercede in prayer, we stand in the gap to mediate with God on behalf of others.

- Supplication is found in the rudimentary lists on prayer in both Ephesians 6:18 and Philippians 4:6. It is a humble and earnest pleading to God for specific requests.

- Petition was made in Luke 22:42, and 1 Peter 5:7 gives the motive for petition—casting our cares on Him.[2]

In light of Philippians 4:6, I would also add "Thanksgiving" to the list.

Worship

The disciples worshipped Christ as He ascended from their final encounter with Him, leaving them in Bethany with the promise of spiritual enabling to carry out His instructions found in Luke 24:50–53. Jesus was worshipped from the time He was born. Most of His worshippers were sincere in their devotion. However, not all worship is acceptable to God.

The New Testament gives us at least two incidents of false intentions in worship. One was when Herod desired to know where the infant Jesus was to be found. He told the wise men that he, too, wanted to worship the new King (Matthew 2:8); but he simply wanted to know His whereabouts so he could eliminate Him as a perceived threat. The other incident of worship with false

---

[2] Knott and MacDonald, *Does It Pay To Pray?*, 5. Used by permission.

intentions is found in Mark 7:6–8, where Jesus describes the existing religious system as one of worship of tradition rather than of God.

When we worship, we are called to worship in Spirit and in truth, as Jesus described to the woman of Samaria in John 4:23–24:

> But the hour cometh, and now is, when the true worshippers shall worship the Father in spirit and in truth: for the Father seeketh such to worship Him. God is a Spirit: and they that worship Him must worship Him in spirit and in truth.

Speaking the names of God is one way to worship Him as a prelude to personal prayer. His names describe His character and His relationship with us. Praise in song or by word and praying praises or verses from Scripture are other ways we can worship during private prayer. We cannot help but recognize the amazing gifts God has given us as His adopted children when we begin with worship. This draws us into a protected mindset in which Satan is loath to enter because the very name of our Lord Jesus Christ acts as a deterrent to his presence. Worship prepares us to hear from God in our innermost being, giving us the strength to intentionally reject distraction. The Holy Spirit is then able to work in us unhindered by the devices of the enemy.

Confession

As John 15:7 tells us, confession is necessary to "abide in Christ." Jesus Himself told His disciples to ask for forgiveness in the so-called "Lord's Prayer" (Matthew 6:9). James exhorted, "Confess your faults one to another, and pray one for another, that ye may be healed" (James 5:16). First John 1:9 says, "If we confess our sins, He is faithful and just to forgive us our sins, and to cleanse us from all unrighteousness." Confession is to agree with God that you have sinned.

While our sins are all cleansed by the blood of Jesus Christ (1 John 1:6), in John 13:9, Jesus Himself uses the metaphor of washing feet to point out that we do need to have our feet washed occasionally from the inevitable "dust" picked up as we walk in an unclean world. In the same way, we need to recognize and eliminate those things in our own lives that do not honor our God.

In other words, in confession, we deal with sin that we have allowed to gain a foothold in our lives to the detriment of our walk with God. Confession includes a plea for forgiveness. It also includes the recognition that God has indeed cleansed us from *all* sin so that we are not bound in any way to disobey God and follow our old nature. We are new creatures in Christ.

Confession and forgiveness for the Christian involves the *intentional* setting aside of those sins (whether from the world, the flesh, or the devil) that hound us and compromise our effectiveness in the calling and giftedness God has given us.

Pleading for Ourselves and Others

In Scripture, intercession, supplication, and petition are used interchangeably in some cases. However, it appears there are differences in the function of each of these, depending on the context. While intercession is spiritual battle in prayer, it may or may not be related to discerning of spirits.

Intercession is described in Ezekiel 22:30–31. When we intercede in prayer, we stand in the gap to mediate with God on behalf of others. In intercession, we agree with God about issues the Holy Spirit brings to mind. While we do not change the purpose of God by intercession, we can influence the action of God. Intercession is a spiritual battle; this is where strongholds are broken, surrendered ground is retaken, and God's righteousness prevails. It is through intercession that we "labor fervently in prayer" as Epaphras did in Colossians 4:12.

Intercession is also the wrestling "against principalities, against powers, against the rulers of the darkness of this world, against spiritual wickedness in high *places"* (Ephesians 6:12). Persistence in prayer is necessary to hold the ground that has been taken in intercession.

Supplication is found in the rudimentary lists on prayer in both Ephesians 6:18 and Philippians 4:6–7. It is a humble and earnest pleading to God for specific requests for others, with thanksgiving. R. A. Torrey contends that, for our Lord Jesus Christ, prayer was not just part of His life on earth; it is also of particular importance in His ministry as our risen Savior. Since Christ intercedes for us with God as our advocate (1 John 2:1), our part is to exercise supplication in the Holy Spirit and for "all saints" (Ephesians 6:18).[3]

Petition was made in Luke 22:42, and 1 Peter 5:7 gives the motive for petition—casting our cares on Him. It is with petition that we pray for ourselves. Each of us knows the private concerns we have within ourselves and for ourselves. Sometimes we are so deeply moved by our needs that we find the Holy Spirit making "intercession for us with groanings too deep for words ... according to the will of God" (Romans 8:26–27) because we have not the words for what we feel we need. This intercession is a spiritual battle and demonstrates part of the scriptural role of the Holy Spirit in prayer. The Holy Spirit teaches us how to pray just as Jesus taught the disciples how to pray. First John 4:13 gives us the evidence of the indwelling Spirit in us by which we know that God dwells in us, and Ephesians 6:18 entreats us to "pray in the Spirit."

This intercession by the Holy Spirit is also a petition on our behalf whether or not we recognize the spiritual battle in our own lives. When we walk fully committed lives in Christ through the Holy Spirit, our desires and needs line up with God's will for us and others we pray for. We also have an advocate in the presence of the Father, "Jesus Christ the righteous" (1 John 2:1). First John 5:14–15 assures us that "this is the confidence that

---

[3] R. A. Torrey, *How to Pray* (New Kensington, PA: Whitaker House, 1984), 5–6.

we have in Him, that, if we ask any thing according to His will, He heareth us: and if we know that He hear us, whatsoever we ask, we know that we have the petitions that we desired of Him."

Philippians 4:6–7 uses both "supplication" and "petition." Being anxious for nothing, the promise of incomprehensible peace is conditional on our "prayer and supplication with thanksgiving" along with making our requests (another word for "petitions") known to God. The context indicates that our supplications for others go hand-in-hand with our petitions for ourselves and are confirmed by gratitude. The human experience is similar throughout the world. Though we do not experience the same needs and events, nor do we react in exactly the same way as others, we can engage in a certain amount of empathy with the recognition of the similarities in the emotional, spiritual, and physical needs that God created in all humans.

Thanksgiving

As seen in Philippians 4:6 and 1 Thessalonians 5:18, the Bible also shows that it is God's will that we express gratitude and thanksgiving in prayer. In the Old Testament, Leviticus and Nehemiah demonstrated specific instructions for thanksgiving sacrifices and job descriptions for people charged with the thanksgiving aspect of worship and prayer. Throughout the Psalms, David frequently expressed thanksgiving, which also validates that thanksgiving needs to be a key part of our worship and prayer.

Verses like Psalm 100:4, "Enter into His gates with thanksgiving, *and* into His courts with praise: be thankful unto Him, *and* bless His name," make it clear that our coming to God in personal prayer, as well as corporate prayer, needs to involve thanksgiving of some kind. After Jesus's ascension, the apostles "were continually in the temple, praising and blessing God" (Luke 24:53). Paul admonished us to "Rejoice evermore. Pray without ceasing. In everything give thanks: for this is the will of God in Christ Jesus concerning you" (1 Thessalonians 5:16–18).

Notice that the passage establishes a relationship of obedience through ceaseless rejoicing, prayer, and thanksgiving for *everything*. This means that, even when we don't feel like it or things look very bleak and hopeless in our lives, we are still called to glorify God in obedience by a prayerful "attitude of gratitude" that pervades everything about our lives. This also means that we are to always express our gratitude to God, not just when things are going well. Lloyd John Ogilvie calls this "thanksliving."[4] It is when we obediently live this way that we are able to access the power of God to stand against the enemy of our souls.

Second Corinthians 4:15–18 affirms the place of thanksgiving in the life of a Christian and the character of our eternal nature as the focus of what happens by God's will in our lives:

---

[4] John Lloyd Ogilvie, *God's Best for My Life* (Eugene, OR: Harvest House Publishing, 1981), 27.

For all things are for your sakes, that the abundant grace might through the thanksgiving of many redound to the glory of God. For which cause we faint not; but though our outward man perish, yet the inward man is renewed day by day. For our light affliction, which is but for a moment, worketh for us a far more exceeding and eternal weight of glory; while we look not at the things which are seen, but at the things which are not seen: for the things which are seen are temporal; but the things which are not seen are eternal.

Thanksgiving on our part for all that God sends our way, and the resultant joy, is a reflection of our understanding that it is for the Glory of God that we exist. Colossians 2:6–7 confirms thanksgiving as the expression of mature Christianity: "As ye have therefore received Christ Jesus the Lord, so walk ye in Him: rooted and built up in Him, and stablished in the faith, as ye have been taught, abounding therein with thanksgiving."

As they stand about the throne worshipping God, even the angels include "thanksgiving" in their list of elements of adoration due to the King of Kings: "Blessing, and glory, and wisdom, and thanksgiving, and honour, and power, and might, be unto our God for ever and ever" (Revelation 7:12).

Everything about our Christianity, including prayer and thanksgiving, requires faith. Just as "without faith it is impossible to please God" (Hebrews 11:6), so too faith is necessary to prayer. Faith informs all of our actions and communications with God as revealed in 1 John 3:22, "And whatsoever we ask, we receive of Him, because we keep His commandments, and do those things that are pleasing in His sight."

First John 5:14–15 further explains, "And this is the confidence that we have in Him, that, if we ask any thing according to His will, He heareth us: and if we know that He hear us, whatsoever we ask, we know that we have the petitions that we desired of Him." Faith is necessary to know He hears us and will answer. Likewise, Mark 11:24 makes belief the condition for a response when we pray, "Therefore, I say unto you, what things so ever ye desire, when ye pray, believe that ye receive them, and ye shall have them."

Even Jesus talked about how crucial faith is in prayer when He said, "Ask, and it shall be given you; seek, and ye shall find; knock, and it shall be opened unto you: for every one that asketh receiveth; and he that seeketh findeth; and to him that knocketh it shall be opened" (Matthew 7:7–8).

James 1:5–6 demonstrates the severity of praying without faith: "If any of you lack wisdom, let him ask of God, that giveth to all men liberally, and upbraids not; and it shall be given him. But let him ask in faith, nothing wavering. For he that wavers is like a wave of the sea driven with the wind and tossed."

Likewise, 1 Thessalonians 5:17 exhorts us to pray without ceasing, an admonition that is even more important for those called to stand in the gap in the midst of battle, the discerner of spirits and the spiritual warrior. Part of "praying without ceasing" is persevering in prayer until the Holy Spirit prompts us to recognize the answer.

Andrew Murray described delayed answer to prayer as an important part of God's "school of faith": "It is to Him a matter of deep importance that His friends on earth should know and fully trust their rich Friend in heaven ... He trains them, in the school of answer delayed, to find out how their perseverance really does prevail, and what the mighty power is they can wield in heaven, if they but set themselves to it ... It is when the answer to prayer does not come and the promise we are most firmly trusting appears to be of no effect, that the trial of faith ... takes place ... Faith, then, takes and holds the promise until it receives the fulfillment of what was claimed as vital truth from the unseen but living God."[5]

Summary

Personal prayer is important to our Christian growth because it is time spent communicating directly with God. It includes worship, confession, intercession, supplication, petition, and thanksgiving. Repeatedly, the Bible stresses the importance of prayer to our walk with God in terms of promised peace, dependence on God, joy, and answered prayer. Faith is necessary for effective prayer, and the more we exercise this concept, the more we recognize our reliance on Him for all that we need.

[5] Murray, *The Believer's School of Prayer,* 52.

CHAPTER TWELVE

About Power Prayer

Intercessory prayer is not the only tool in the hand of one gifted in discerning of spirits. The power prayer commands Satan and his emissaries to depart in Jesus's name outright, and it is often a necessary procedure in spiritual warfare. The Bible warns us about "vain repetitions," and we need to be wary of falling into the trap of using pronouncements as if they were magic incantations, however. We do not deal in magic.

Authority from Jesus Christ

When power prayer is used, the Christian exercises the authority over principalities and powers given to us by Jesus Christ Himself. Romans 8:37–39 reminds us:

> … in all these things we are more than conquerors through Him that loved us. For I am persuaded, that neither death, nor life, nor angels, nor principalities, nor powers,

nor things present, nor things to come, nor height, nor depth, nor any other creature, shall be able to separate us from the love of God, which is in Christ Jesus our Lord.

Furthermore, 1 John 5:4–5 says, "For whatsoever is born of God overcometh the world: and this is the victory that overcometh the world, even our faith. Who is he that overcometh the world, but he that believeth that Jesus is the Son of God?"

When I power pray, I follow the basic pattern presented by Neil Anderson[1] with reminders to the enemy that we belong to the King of Kings and Satan has no authority over God's people. It is said out loud or whispered. Satan is not able to directly read our thoughts or hear our authoritative commands unless they are said aloud.[2] According to Anderson, "He is under no obligation to obey your thoughts. Only God has complete knowledge of your mind."[3]

Usually, the prayer sounds something like this: "In Jesus's name and by the Blood of Jesus Christ, I com-

---

[1] See chapter 10 for more information on power prayer.

[2] Because Satan is an angel, and angels are created beings, he is not omniscient and he is not omnipresent as God is. The incident in Daniel 10 gives evidence that angels cannot be in more than one place at a time. First Peter 1:12, Ephesians 3:10, and 1 Corinthians 11:10 seem to point to our relationship to God as a mystery to the angels (and demons by association), who appear to lack understanding of salvation because it does not pertain to them. Because of this evidence of limitation among God's highest created beings, I believe that the enemy cannot "hear" our prayers or read our thoughts. He can, apparently, "read" the spiritual activity surrounding us. And he can somehow suggest temptations and inappropriate thoughts to us. However, I believe our conversations with God are private unless they are spoken aloud.

[3] Anderson, *The Bondage Breaker,* 186.

mand you, Satan, and your emissaries, to leave this place. You have no authority here. We belong to the Lord Jesus Christ, King of Kings and Lord of Lords."

I also pray for a hedge of protection from God and call upon Him to bind the enemy in that place. Frequently, God gives me the names and circumstances of individuals for whom I need to pray directly. These may be Christians who have inadvertently or unknowingly brought spiritual conflict into the sanctuary.

Holy Spirit-Led Perception

As mentioned earlier, there are times when I experience the recognition of spiritual conflict outside the congregation of believers. Each instance is different, but each time it is the perception of an intrusion into or from the spiritual realm—a recognition of the need to stand in the gap against the enemy. Furthermore, the first call is to prayer, and God leads from there, showing me most often that I need to continue with intercessory prayer for those involved. Occasionally, the action I am led to is to share the gospel in that place. At other times, it is a fleeting experience, leaving me with no other recourse than to continue to pray for the individuals involved until a word from the Lord Jesus Christ indicates a cessation of prayer on that subject.

There are those who would suggest that the spiritual discerner is judging based on a subjective quantity called "feeling." I disagree in that it is God-given insight that prompts ministry in prayer, exhortation, or spiritual warfare. For the discerner of spirits, there is a definite difference between merely emotional feelings and the experience of recognizing spiritual activity. Part of it is the unexplainable nature of many of our encounters as discerners. Another factor is the suddenness with which we are confronted by the sense of evil activity. Further, the authentication of the gift is in the God-given, God-directed, and God-glorifying nature of the outcomes of the gift, as well as the implicit inclusion of the gift in the scriptural record.

There are times when God calls me to pray for people I have never met, people's names I have heard (i.e., celebrities or missionaries), even when they are not in the news. I suspect that this part of prayer is more widespread than just among people who are gifted in discerning of spirits. In corporate church prayer, we often pray for people who are in the news because of tragic circumstances or high-profile political positions. Through the work of the Holy Spirit, God brings circumstances in need of prayer to the attention of His people in general. The difference is that discerning of spirits deals specifically with direct, interactive spiritual warfare.

To stand in the gap as a gatekeeper on behalf of any church body is a calling and a gifting that must come from our Lord Jesus Christ and must be powered by the Holy Spirit. The continual awareness of the spiritual realm is not a gift after which I sought, but neither is it something I would willingly change. God grows each of us in unique ways, differing according to His perfect will in our creation and in our refining as His children. First Corinthians 12 makes it clear that God gives diverse gifts, placing His people in His Church for His purposes. Under the singular direction of the Spirit of God, He uses this diversity of gifts to form a fully functional body to represent Him, in His own ways, on Earth. It is important that each believer seek to understand what God has gifted and called him or her to do according to God's timing and placement.

Summary

Power prayer is the direct, confrontational commanding away of evil spirits, backed by God's authority, in the name of and by the blood of our Lord Jesus Christ. In order to be effective, it requires faith to recognize the authority we have over Satan and his demons through our Lord Jesus Christ.

CHAPTER THIRTEEN

Counterfeits of Spiritual Discernment

The spiritual gift of "discerning of spirits" is undeniably misunderstood, and it is widely counterfeited by Satan to confuse the truly God-given gift with occult imitations of its characteristics in the minds of many people.

Differentiating the Source

God-given discerning of spirits gives as clear a picture of the continuous but physically unseen spiritual battle as humans are able to perceive. While all of the spiritual gifts can be imitated and are frequently accepted in non-Christians, discerning of spirits is especially so. Non-Christians who have the ability to perceive spiritual events do so through demonic power. Because of this presence of counterfeits, the God-given gift can seem bizarre to Christians not gifted in this way, to the point of refusal to accept discerning-of-spirit outcomes in their fellow Christians.

A largely unrecognized aspect of the spiritual gift of discerning of spirits is its scope beyond the identification of false spirits that influence false teachers and prophets. It also includes the perception of spiritual and demonic activity in both individuals and churches. Because of the subtlety and perniciousness of demonic activity, people gifted to recognize and understand spiritual activity in both arenas are necessary to the health of the modern Church.

For the same reason, spiritual discerners and church leadership alike need to verify the source of the ability to recognize and interact with spiritual events (1 John 4:1–4). If Jesus Christ is not the source, then it is not a gift of the Holy Spirit but a device of Satan himself to divert God's people.

Furthermore, it is not a "family gift" passed from generation to generation like many occult practices are. There are those who would suggest that the gift of discerning of spirits is inherited.

This fits with the demonstration of a familiar spirit invited into the family through sin in past generations as seen in Exodus 34:7.

In discerning false teachers and prophets, the true "plumb-bob" is Scripture with which to line up questionable input. Based on this, warnings can be made to the churches, and the ideal outcome is that those churches be set aright. It is sad that, even with scriptural confirmation, so many congregations of believers disregard the warnings of their God-given discernment personnel. These people are watchdogs for each church's benefit. To ignore their counsel could result in a church split by divisions that devastate Christian lives and seriously compromise the testimony of God to the world.

Discerning of spirits, however, does not carry with it as clear a definition of right and wrong as false teaching and prophecy. The gifting is the same kind of sensation we relate to as hearing a word from God. When we "hear" the voice of God, it is usually exclusively a spiritual event, understood only by the individual and requiring verification with Scripture to authenticate its contents. Discerning of spirits is, in large part, experiential and, therefore, comes with much danger of being skewed by individual schema and the subtlety of the devil.

There are those who would partake of this power without the power of Jesus behind their actions. Matthew 7:15–23 tells of counterfeit miracles done in Jesus's name by false prophets described as "ravening wolves" in sheep's clothing; but in the final judgment day they will be told, "I never knew you: depart from me ye that work iniquity" (Matthew 7:23).

Acts 8:18–24 records the story of Simon the Sorcerer's false conversion. While Simon accepted the praise of the people and their declarations of his power as coming from God, he was using "sorcery" to "bewitch" the people with Satanic lies. He seemed to demonstrate faith in his acceptance of the Lord Jesus Christ as Savior, even to the point of joining the ministry of the apostles. Later on, it is revealed that he had misunderstood the true power of God behind these miracles. Thinking it something of man's invention, a matter of contrived magic like his own talents were, he offered money for the authority to grant the Holy Spirit as he saw the apostles doing. Peter warned him to repent of his wickedness, calling it a "bond of iniquity" in verse 23.

By trying to buy an apostolic position, he revealed clearly that he was still in bondage to Satan and never truly accepted salvation by faith.

Counterfeit Modes

There are a variety of ways that the devil misconstrues the spiritual interaction of the gift of discerning of spirits. In 2 Corinthians 11:13–15, Paul gives us insight into an aspect of Satan and his demons by which Satan transforms himself into an angel of light: "Therefore, it is no great thing if his ministers also be transformed as the ministers of righteousness: whose end shall be according to their works" (2 Corinthians 11:15).

First Peter 5:8–9 exhorts us not only to sobriety and vigilance but also to resist our adversary, the devil, who, "as a roaring lion, walketh about, seeking whom he may devour: Whom resist steadfast in the faith, knowing that the same afflictions are accomplished in your brethren that are in the world."

Deuteronomy 18:9–12 cites divination, an observer of times, an enchanter, a witch, a charmer, a consulter with familiar spirits, a wizard, and a necromancer as abominations to the Lord. These are listed alongside heinous actions of human sacrifice as forbidden actions. They are given as reasons for the people of Israel to be driven from the land. God calls us, as He called Israel, to holiness unto Him. To do these things that are condemned by God is to step into sin and compromise with the prevailing world system.

Divination involves conversation with the spirit world and generally requires a resident demon. Besides establishing complete power over the host, it is a satanic mimicry of both the Spirit-granted gift of prophecy and of discerning of spirits in that it is an attempt to demonstrate spiritually generated knowledge of the future. Acts 16:16–18 tells of the spirit of divination in the slave woman who followed Paul:

> And it came to pass, as we went to prayer, a certain damsel possessed with a spirit of divination met us, which brought her masters much gain by soothsaying: the same followed Paul and us, and cried, saying, "These men are the servants of the most high God, which shew unto us the way of salvation."
>
> And this did she many days. But Paul, being grieved, turned and said to the spirit, "I command thee in the name of Jesus Christ to come out of her." And he came out the same hour.

An observer of times would be akin to an astrologer who practices divination using the configurations of the planets and stars to predict the future. A necromancer consulted the dead and a consulter of spirits sought out demons for information in order to divine the future.

At best, these are a mockery based on lies in that neither demons nor Satan, which are all created beings, have the prescience (insight into the future) that God has. While the spiritual discerner does not practice foretelling, God does occasionally warn us of coming spiritual conflict. Sometimes it is through a kind of spiritual "chatter," activity that the discerner recognizes as escalating towards a conflict. At other times, God allows the discerner to sense or see exactly what the demonic hordes are up to and how they manipulate the participants.

An enchanter, a witch, a charmer, and a wizard use spells, incantations, and magic to invoke the power of the spirit world to achieve supernatural effects in the physical world. As Christians, we have the power in Jesus's name to command demonic forces away, even to the point of banishing satanic minions from those they seek to enslave (Mark 5:1–13; 16:17). The supernatural is God's venue, and it is sin to attempt to control anything in the spiritual realm outside of His power and will.

Historically, the practice of mimicking God-initiated miracles occurred as far back as Moses's and Aaron's confrontation with Pharaoh in Exodus 7. Pharaoh called his magicians and sorcerers, who were able to reproduce some of the miracles done by Moses and Aaron, apparently through demonic power. While the magicians of Egypt were able to change their rods to snakes and show red water, it is not clear by what means they did this.

They also brought frogs up from the Nile. Whether by some trick of the occult or what, we do not know. However, they could not stop the plagues, nor could they magically make the consequences of the plagues disappear. Try as he did to refute the impotence of his court magicians, Pharaoh himself knew that Jehovah was the author and finisher of the plagues and finally called upon Moses to plead for God's intervention.

Beware!

Those particularly gifted in discerning of spirits must beware of two components of spiritual warfare. First, we are highly susceptible to deviation into wrong motivation from selfishness and pride. As stated above, any attempt to control, deviate from, or comply with one's own agenda with regard to dealing with the supernatural is sin.

Second, many Christians misunderstand and question the origin of the gift because they have never experienced it. This can easily be a source of doubt and discouragement for a Christian who is not fully grounded in Christ. What we do as discerners of spirits, as with all of the gifts of the Holy Spirit, must be done in faith.

While all of the biblical spiritual gifts have their imitations in Satan's kingdom, those with the spiritual gift of discerning of spirits are especially exposed to this for four reasons.

First, this gift puts one on the very frontlines of the battle, in Satan's face, as it were. Remember, this person is the "gatekeeper," the one who stands in the gap, actively repelling the enemy's advances at the very point the wall is broken. As spiritual radar operators, those gifted in discerning of spirits are the first to perceive and recognize the approaching enemy. There is a tremendous malevolent weight on one's spirit in the midst of these battles that can be overwhelming. As mentioned before, God graciously "cocoons" us upon request when we find ourselves beleaguered by the enemy. This frees us to focus on prayer, unburdened of the need to "swing the sword" at the same time.

Second, the characteristics of this gift are so easily imitated and drawn from a source other than God because they are exclusively experienced on a spiritual level, occasionally crossing over into being physically sensed, a phenomenon explored earlier in this book. One hears so often of non-believers with special "gifts" in the areas of extra-sensory perception, mind reading, and ready access to the spirit world. These gifts masquerade as marvels of individual heritage, but they are generated in the pit of hell (Deuteronomy 18:9–14). Their power and sponsorship are derived from demons.

The Christian who is truly gifted with discerning of spirits from the Holy Spirit, however, experiences the genuine article. There are Christian writers who proclaim that *anything* that smacks of these abilities is to be shunned. And yet the supernatural sensation of recognizing spiritual conflict and the presence of evil is perception outside of the physical senses (i.e., in the realm of the supernatural). God gives insight into the "state of mind" of others. While not a mind-reading experience, it is a sense of the spiritual state and influence in which that person exists. The difference is that the spiritual gift of discerning of spirits is God-given, God-directed, and God-glorifying. This is critical to remember.

The one so gifted has to constantly be on guard so as not to interpret input over and above God's direction. The line between godly and ungodly use of this gift is so fine that it would be very easy to stray into unholy ground through selfishness and pride. Dr. Stieglitz says that he often has to tell those of us with this gift not to interpret the information we receive in discerning-of-spirit events. Instead, we need to relay the information to our spiritual leaders or authority and let them interpret and decide what to do with it. The military analogy holds that the radar operator simply transfers information for his superior officers to use for tactical advantage in battle. A medical analogy would be the technician who collects data using a CT scan or MRI to send to a doctor who then interprets the findings in order to develop a diagnostic strategy.

Third, because Satan does not want this warrior to be effective, he makes this look so bizarre by his parodies of the gifts that other Christians deny the power of God behind true discerning of spirits, thereby discounting credibility for one gifted in this way. With the spiritual gift of discerning of spirits comes a unique glimpse into the spiritual realm that is not generally understood or sensed by other Christians. The resultant outpouring of prayer and strengthening of God's angelic host defeat satanic incursions. Attempts to distract the gatekeeper from his or her God-given post include introducing seeds of doubt from within and denigration by others from without. Therefore, it is very important that we, as spiritual discerners, strengthen ourselves in the Word of God and keep pressing forward in prayer.

In large part, the misunderstood nature of spiritual warfare comes from the Western culture in which we live. In previous generations, many Western Christians were taught that the dispensations of miraculous events were past and that spiritual content should be approached with rational arguments instead of demonstrations of the power of God. In recent times, a lack of understanding resulting from secular interest in spiritual matters has caused confusion for Christians with little doctrinal background. The only church involvement many people experience has been based largely on emotional manipulations without biblical rationale. They are not equipped to discern either false teaching and prophecy or the presence of spiritual conflict.

Christian churches now play host to both generational and equally erroneous positions; on the one hand, there are those who disbelieve the gifting because it lacks a rational explanation and, on the other hand, there are those who can't tell the difference and believe "it's all good."

From my perspective regarding the subtlety of Satan's attacks, I am inclined to favor a more moderate road. Having experienced the power and disturbance of spiritually discerned events, both holy and unholy, I understand the validity of supernatural occurrences without the need for intellectual rationale. By the same token, I know that it is not "all good"; the Bible makes it very clear that Satan is our enemy and seeks constantly to devour us. I am willing to endure censure because this position at least gives credence to a persistent spiritual conflict.

Fourth, being a gatekeeper can be a very isolating ministry because the events and subsequent actions are spiritual and supernatural; therefore, they are hidden from the awareness of other people. Furthermore, the gatekeeper is sometimes considered a marginal and lethargic church member because he or she may not have the giftedness or the energy to participate in more public ministries. I have found it necessary to renew in solitude because I personally need a lot of time alone with the Lord to regain strength sapped from me by these unseen battles. This is an enigma of the job God has granted discerners of spirits, requiring wisdom in order to achieve a delicate balance. Without this time alone, the gatekeeper could easily become discouraged because of exhaustion. Yet, with the need for time alone, discouragement could also come from a lack of meaningful fellowship with other believers.

Although we all live in a dualistic world of tangible (natural) and intangible (supernatural) factors, the discerner of spirits is constantly aware of the spiritual realm in ways that make the journey a unique adventure. Because this gift has to do exclusively with an abstract, ethereal plane, accountability is not the same as for those with other gifts. All of the other spiritual gifts are visible by the actions that emanate from those so gifted: prophets prophesy, teachers teach, preachers preach, and helpers help. Accountability in the discerning of spirits has more to do with its effects on the one so gifted (i.e., the outcomes of the gift rather than on observance of the gift in action).

As for all of the gifts of the Spirit, our pastors or designated church authorities are the primary source of spiritual accountability. Each of us who understands what we do and the importance of this gift needs to establish a support team for accountability and prayer. For instance, it has been very beneficial to be able to talk freely with my husband about this gift.

While he does not experience it firsthand, he has seen its effects on me and acknowledges the validity of the ministry that is performed as a result of it. God's provision of my husband's willingness to be the necessary support and guardian for the course God has set for me is an important aspect of the giftedness God has granted me.

Summary

Christians who have never experienced the kind of perception and confrontation with the spiritual realm like those gifted in discerning of spirits encounter, find accounts of such events disturbing and bizarre. In part, this is because Satan "the Subtle" has very carefully crafted counterfeits in all aspects of discerning of spirits in order to denigrate a gift that so blatantly exposes his schemes to the Christian community.

The discerner of spirits must always be on guard to make sure his or her gift is not sidetracked because of the sins of selfishness and pride. We serve God joyfully with a gift that is crucial to the protection of God's people and to the spread of the gospel in a world under the usurper's domination. The Holy Spirit must power all that we do, and the outcomes must be God-given, God-directed, and God-glorifying.

CHAPTER FOURTEEN

Discerning Angelic Activity

First Corinthians describes the gift of "discerning of spirits" as a classification into which angelic activity belongs. During a recent conversation, Dr. Stieglitz reminded me that if I am able to sense the activity of *fallen* angels, then it follows that I should also be able to sense the activity of *holy* angels.

Answered Prayer

In John 4:24, God is described as "a Spirit: and they that worship Him must worship Him in spirit and in truth." I began to ask God to give me a sense of the holy angels around me, as well as that of other spirits I already perceive.

At first, I had not been able to recognize any. However, when the revelation came some weeks later, it was not just one angel but several. When it did happen, it took my breath away and was, in its own way, almost as disturbing as the presence of demonic activity.

For those of us who are spiritually gifted to "discern spirits," worship at church is more often than not about a calling rather than a comfort zone. Even so, it surprised me that even the recognition of angelic activity was initially so uncomfortable and powerful, at least according to my own experience. Perhaps it is that I have grown used to the "cocoon" protection of the Lord and that I like that soft, comfortable place too much. Another discerner of spirits agreed with me that we are occasionally able to conveniently "turn our gift off."

On Sunday mornings during services, I generally spend most of my time in the outer room at church praying. That day, I was in my seat as our worship team played the initial set. I watched through a nearby window as a basketball team in jogging suits approached our front door. I later learned that they were from a Christian university some distance away and had come to our town for a tournament sponsored by the local community college. I knew my angels had arrived with this team.

When they entered the building, I was blown away with an enormous sense of joy I don't recall ever having felt before. I was able to worship God during that worship service in a way that is normally blocked for me because of the discerning of spirits gift in action during the meetings of our church. I recognized the difference in the spiritual disturbance they caused because I was prompted to praise God.

Whereas a demonic presence causes a sense of despair and an intense desire to run from the place, the experience of angels was remarkably different. This was clearly an extraordinary visitation that left me weeping for sheer joy throughout the service. Even as I write, I find myself with tears in my eyes and a sense of amazement at what happened. It was also evident that many others in our congregation who normally do not "discern spirits" knew that there was a difference in the worship that morning.

There are two possibilities that I can think of for this amazing demonstration from God. The first is that God had indeed answered my prayer and shown me angelic activity previously, but I had not recognized it because I was not trained to recognize angels as I had been trained to recognize demonic activity. The second possibility is that He did not show me angelic activity until He revealed clearly and with power what the experience of discerning the presence of angels is like. Such a powerful demonstration of the angelic presence awakened within me what would immediately recognize similar activity in the future.

The Character and Function of Angels

Have you ever wondered why so many times the first thing an angel says when he shows up in Scripture is "fear not"? Biblical accounts describe visible angels (angels who have a temporary physical form) as amazing, fearsome creatures. We are unaccustomed to the spiritual glory that is visible when we see them with physical eyes, but that is readily discerned by those gifted in discerning of spirits. God Himself allowed Moses to see Him only from the back because a man cannot look on the face of God and live. Even with that view of God, Moses was prompted to fall on his knees and worship. Exodus 24:17 also reveals, "The sight of the glory of the LORD was like devouring fire on the top of the mount in the eyes of the children of Israel."

His messengers coming to us from the presence of God carry with them the glory of His presence. Like Moses's shining face, a physical remnant apparently shines through. In Acts 12:7, it is reported that when the angel came to release Peter from prison, a light shone. It doesn't say that it came from the angel, but where else would the light come from in the middle of the night?

By the creative power of God, angels also took physical form to appear as men to visit Abraham with the Lord in Genesis 18.[1] Not only does the text say that it was the Lord who visited Abraham, but also, none of the beings present objected to Abraham bowing before the Lord as they would have if He were only an angel. In Hebrews 13, we are exhorted to be hospitable to strangers so that we don't miss entertaining "angels unawares." The presence of angels usually goes

---

[1] Strong, *Strong's Exhaustive Concordance of the Bible Together with Dictionaries of the Hebrew and Greek Words of the Original*, "Hebrew and Chaldee Dictionary," 47. KJV uses "LORD" to designate who was visiting Abraham. The capitalized "LORD" in English denotes the translation of the Hebrew word frequently pronounced "Yahweh" by English speakers. It is translated "Self-Existent or Eternal; Jehovah, Jewish national name of God: Jehovah, the Lord."

unremarked by humans. Angels, in their natural form, are invisible to human eyes because they are spirit, not flesh. However, God occasionally allows us to see them. Angels don't always appear as bigger than life when they take physical form.

Except in the garden of Eden, when Satan appeared in the form of a snake, angels do not appear as animals. There is no other place in the Bible that implies that even demons take the form of animals.[2] God used animals in a variety of services, including the ravens that were commanded to feed Elijah at the brook Cherith in 1 Kings 17 as well as the bears that killed the children who had mocked Elisha in 2 Kings 3. At Gadara, Jesus sent the demons into swine; the demons did not take the form of animals from something other than swine. God is the only one who can create form from formlessness or change the form of a created being.

Like demons, angels are created beings and not to be worshipped in any way. They are part of the "host of heaven" who worship God in Nehemiah 9:6. The writer of Hebrews makes the point that Jesus Christ was, unlike the angels, called God's Son and also called God (as in "Thy throne, Oh God, is for ever and ever" from Hebrews 1:8). When Jesus Christ was born into the world, the heavenly Father proclaimed, "let all the angels of God worship Him" (Hebrews 1:6).

Angels do not share God's supernatural attributes; in other words, they are not omniscient, omnipotent,

---

[2] Note the difference in syntax between "taking the form" of an animal and "possession" of an existing animal for demonic use.

or omnipresent. Though they were created, they do not die, marry, or partake in salvation. They are wise, holy, submissive, and humble, and so numerous as to be uncountable by human standards. The angels, both those who are in service to God and those who have fallen and serve the enemy of our souls (demons), are above man in power and might. But according to 1 Corinthians 6:3, God's saints, those who believe the gospel of the cross of Jesus Christ unto salvation, will judge angels.

The job of angels is to obey the will of God, to communicate His messages, and to implement His plans. Angels are called "holy" (Matthew 25:31) and "elect" (1 Timothy 5:21), which means they are chosen and set apart for the exclusive use of God. In obedience to God, they act as ministering spirits as seen when an angel fed Elijah under the juniper tree in 1 Kings 19 and when the beggar at the rich man's table was carried by angels to Abraham's bosom when he died in Luke 16. They also ministered to Jesus Christ during His earthly ministry (Matthew 4:11). They are subject to Christ (1 Peter 3:22), as well as foreseen to be attending Him at His second coming (Matthew 25:31).

Angels communicate the will of God, as was shown in the prophetic progressions of Daniel 8–12. They also make important announcements like the conception of John and of Jesus in the gospel of Luke 1 and 2, the birth of Christ in Luke 2, His resurrection in Matthew 28, and His ascension and second coming in Acts 1. In addition, they are sent to accomplish God's will, as in Matthew 13:41 and 24:31.

Angels do not participate in salvation but "desire to look into [salvation]" (1 Peter 1:12). Salvation is a mystery to them, but they rejoice over the repentance of a sinner as seen in Luke 15:7 and 10. It is through those of us who know Jesus Christ as Savior that the angels observe and are able to know "the manifold wisdom of God" (Ephesians 3:9–10).

The angels are set up in a hierarchy with differing ranks, including an Archangel named Michael, angels under Michael's command who will fight the dragon and his angels (Revelation 12:7), and Seraphim who guard the throne of God (Isaiah 6:1–2). Besides those who ministered directly to the Lord Jesus Christ (Matthew 4:11), there are also those who protect the children of God as was described in Daniel 6 and Acts 12.

There are angels who worship God continually (Psalm 148; Isaiah 6; Revelation 4). Angelic worship and celebration of God occurred especially at key historical events. They sang at creation (Job 38:7) and at Christ's birth (Luke 2:13–14). They will also glorify God before the opening of the Seal Judgments (Revelation 15) and before the opening of the Seventh Seal (Revelation 7).

The Logistics of Divine Intervention

When I was growing up, any mention of miraculous interventions by angels was viewed with skepticism. According to most of the Christians around me, those things only happened in the Bible, and their function was to confirm the power behind salvation in our Lord

Jesus Christ. The prevailing thought was that, since they are written down, we have the record so we no longer need to see miraculous events. The elders in my childhood church believed that anything "supernatural" in modern times was considered demonic in origin. It has been my personal experience, however, that God still works miracles and answers prayer in amazing ways. Those of us gifted in "discerning of spirits" are privileged to readily recognize the miraculous because of our God-given sensitivity to perceive spiritual events.

As He promised, God has not changed. He still works in the world today as He did in the Bible. When He protected His people in response to prayer, occasionally, it was by showing earth-bound senses a glimpse into the eternal, spiritual sphere that mortal man cannot access without supernatural intervention by Almighty God. In 2 Kings 7, for instance, enemy ears heard the sound of a mighty army with horses and chariots that did not exist in the physical world. It frightened them into a mad exodus, leaving their camp open for some Jewish lepers to find empty and the subsequent occupation by Jewish troops.

The ability for a discerner of spirits to hear God's voice of direction within and to sense spiritual conflict is, in fact, miraculous. It requires a divinely orchestrated crossover between the spiritual and physical realms, an open door, if you will, between two incompatible planes. The spiritual realm has God-set boundaries that God has chosen not to reveal to us; it goes beyond the tangible and is not bound in the same way as the physical world. The physical, on the other hand, is bound by both time and space. The tangibles of the physical are not the same as the tangibles of the spiritual. Indeed, what is tangible in the physical world may be abstract in the spiritual,[3] just as what is abstract in the spiritual world is tangible in the physical world. It is only by the power of the Creator, God Himself, that discerning of spirits is possible.

Jesus gave us a small picture of the partition between the physical and the spiritual in the story of the rich man and the beggar, Lazarus, in Luke 16. Both the rich man and Lazarus died.

The rich man was sent to Hades, and Lazarus was sent to "Abraham's bosom." This incident was recounted before Jesus died, was buried, rose again, and ascended. Therefore, He had not yet "led captivity captive"[4] (Psalm 68:18). Perhaps it was part of the torture of Hades to be able to see what could have been. In any case, having requested aid from Lazarus, the rich man was denied access to even the briefest respite.

It appears that the people in "Abraham's bosom" were not even aware of their counterparts in Hades. But for some reason, it was Abraham through whom the rich man was allowed to communicate. Abraham

---

[3] As noted in chapter 5, in the spiritual realm there seems to be a tangible factor to words, abstract concepts in the physical world. Jesus is called "the Word" in John 1, and by "the Word" all things were made. In the physical world, using words, not written but spoken, cannot by any stretch of the imagination create something tangible.

[4] MacDonald, *Believers Bible Commentary New Testament*, 651. "Paul applies verse 18 to the Ascension of Christ (Ephesians 4:8–10). When Christ ascended from earth to heaven, He led captivity captive, that is, He triumphed gloriously over His foes and gave gifts to men."

told the rich man that there was a "great gulf fixed: so that they that would pass from hence to you cannot; neither can they pass to us that would come from thence" (Luke 16:26).

When Abraham also said that the raising of Lazarus from the dead would not sway the rich man's brothers to godliness, it was in terms of the existence of the written Word of God. There is no mention that the return of one from God's presence would be impossible. Nevertheless, reentering time and space from eternity (spiritual realms) requires divine intervention. Jesus Christ Himself raised Lazarus of Bethany from the dead in John 11. However, Christ is the only one who ever rose from the dead on His own (John 2:19–22). It is only by God's will that spiritual forces are rendered visible to the physical realm.

Anecdotal Evidence of Angels in the World

Stories of angelic intervention are not confined to the Bible. Incidents have been documented by a variety of modern missionaries and writers. Marie Monson, a Norwegian missionary to China during the early twentieth century, related many instances of discerning of spirits. Many of her stories of divine intervention consist of discerning-of-spirit events that sound like when Elisha asked God to show his servant the spiritual forces surrounding them.

For instance, when a Communist army was approaching a city where she was visiting, the Christians in that city met periodically during the day to pray. An officer from the approaching troop later asked one of the church members about the double wall around the city and the strange sentinels standing on the outer wall. There was only one physical wall around that city, and only a handful of civil defense guards had been standing watch on it.[5] Godless soldiers, not recognizing the spiritual nature of the God-created vision they saw, interpreted it in the only way they could; they perceived an additional wall and intimidating sentinels in such a way that the city was protected. Undeniably, "The angel of the Lord encamps round about them that fear Him, and delivers them" (Psalm 34:7).

Among her recollections, Miss Monson also wrote of a time when local soldiers were rebelling because their general had no money to pay them. He had told them they could loot the city one night in lieu of pay. Many fearful neighbors came to the mission compound for protection, each carrying a small bundle of valuables. The Chinese Christians in the compound took full advantage of the time with the terrified townspeople, sharing the gospel and demonstrating the peace of God that passes understanding. While shooting and noise were heard throughout the night and bullets whizzed overhead when the compound occupants tried to cross the open courtyard, no soldiers visited their building. The next day, a number of neighbors who had stayed in their

---

[5] Marie Monson, *A Present Help: Standing on the Promises of God* (Santa Ana, CA: Calvary Chapel Publishing, 2008), 54–55.

homes came to ask if they could stay in the compound next time there was trouble. They had perceived a protection there that they had found nowhere else.[6]

Numerous neighbors had seen four soldiers guarding the place whom they thought had been sent by the General. When asked for further details, they said they could only see silhouettes but that they were the tallest soldiers they had ever seen, and their faces, those of foreigners who were not Chinese, glowed. Later, another man came in asking who had been standing on the east veranda, the other side of the compound, through the night. No human had been out on the veranda, but this man had seen "many people" there when he had looked several times during the night. The angels sent to protect the mission were not seen by the Christians there. There was a two-fold result from the event—not only were the Christians protected, but also many doors were open to share the gospel with unsaved townspeople.

Carl Knott and William MacDonald told the story of a missionary and his helper returning with money for his hospital. Being on foot, the missionary said they would camp out on a nearby hill when night fell.

"But there are bandits in these parts," his companion answered. "What about the money?"

"The money is for God's work; we will ask Him to take care of it," was the reply. So, after praying together, they went to sleep. The next morning, they found both themselves and God's money safe.

[6] Monson, Ibid., 36–40.

Months passed and a brigand chief was brought to the hospital. While receiving treatment he asked: "Did you go to [such-and-such] city a little while ago and bring back some money?"

"Yes!"

"Did you camp on a little hill with soldiers guarding you?"

"We camped on a hill, but had no soldiers guarding us."

"Oh, but you did!" replied the brigand. "We went to rob you, but were afraid of the twenty-seven soldiers!"

The rest of the account came out some months later when the story was related in a meeting in England. "One who was present told the speaker, 'But we had a prayer meeting on that night, I remember,' and looking at his diary, he added, 'and there were twenty-seven of us present.'"[7]

For each person praying, there had been an angel guarding the missionary and his companion. As with Marie Monson's experience, it was the brigands who were given a special discerning of spirits that night. However, they lacked understanding that what they saw was a spiritual manifestation because they were spiritually dead.

Kevin Dyer wrote of miraculous intervention while he headed up a courier ministry to believers in Eastern

---

[7] Knott and MacDonald, *Does It Pay To Pray?*, 37–38. Used by permission.

European communist countries during the latter part of the twentieth century. The team delivered needed food and supplies to pastors of persecuted churches, as well as Bibles and other Christian literature translated into the language of each country they visited.

He told of one particularly difficult border crossing, after which authorities followed the team for many miles. Instead of going directly to the pre-arranged drop-off point, they took alternate routes, trying to lose their pursuers. When they finally felt they were free of them, they proceeded to the church.

When they pulled into the yard, the believers shut the gate behind them and said, "You must have had a difficult time."

"Yes," they replied, "how did you know?"

"Well, when you drove in, we saw two angels, one sitting on each side of the front of the car, and we knew God had protected you."[8]

We are amazed when we hear of these relatively recent events in which human beings are allowed a glimpse of angels and demons from outside tangible perceptions. Reading of occurrences like these in the Bible renders credible the possibilities of similar incidents. But having them confirmed in modern times shows us God's authority, plans, and perfect timing in a way that nothing else could.

---

[8] Kevin G. Dyer, *Life Miracles* (Hoffman Estates, IL: Bright hope International, 2010), 13. Used by permission.

Summary

It is logical that discerners of spirits can sense the presence and activity of angels, as well as demons. The function of angels is to obey the will of God. They are created beings, messengers, warriors, and worshippers, among other attributes. When they appear as physical beings, they usually look like fearsome creatures to the humans who see them. Their presence is not exclusive to biblical accounts; there are also many modern accounts in which angels have been seen in physical form.

CHAPTER FIFTEEN

Marriage, Family, and the Discerner of Spirits

As I mentioned before, my husband is an important part of the support and accountability for my gift. It has been beneficial to be able to talk freely with him about my experiences. While he does not experience it firsthand, he has seen its effects on me and, in turn, has grown in his understanding of the gift, acknowledging the validity of the ministry that is performed as a result of it.

While all marital relationships should be "personal fan clubs," each for the other, there is a unique spousal partnership when discerning of spirits is a part of the equation. God's provision of my husband's willingness to be the protective guardian for the course He has set for me is a key aspect of my discerning-of-spirits experience.

The Necessity of Support and Accountability

As a discerner of spirits, I find that I am particularly sensitive to the spiritual attachments of the people around me. When we were much younger and did not understand the ramifications of my particular gift set, my husband frequently found me agitated when he arrived home from work. Both of us felt frustrated because I couldn't tell him what was wrong. I didn't know myself why I was so overwhelmed. Now I understand the nature of many of my experiences as spiritual attacks taking place in my home. My husband usually recognized the need to go to prayer about my struggles, even though he didn't understand them as spiritual discernment events at the time.

A pastor who has the gift of discerning of spirits tells me that his wife keeps his life uncluttered for him so he can focus on the important aspects of both his ministry and his giftedness in discerning. By "uncluttered," he did not necessarily mean physical clutter but the taking on of niggling aspects of their life that she can transact without his intervention, leaving him free to focus on the priorities of his home and church. While this is an important function for the wife of any active minister of God as his helpmeet, it is especially so in the life of a discerner of spirits. They are two halves of one whole ministering together—she, as the protective guardian of her husband's orderly routine and peaceful home, and he, as the administrator of both home and church.

Not every discerner of spirits has this kind of support in the home. In a home that is Christ-centered, this is something that needs to be openly discussed, instructed, and agreed upon by the family members involved, relying on the Holy Spirit to teach them. It might be your spouse, parents, siblings, or adult children, depending upon your situation. These people know you better than anyone else and, with experience, can more readily recognize what the struggle looks like in you. They can help you by objectively reminding you of the precepts of what God calls you to do as a discerner of spirits and by praying with you and for you. They can also hold you accountable to Scripture in connection with your gift, helping you to recognize if you are moving toward pride or selfishness in the exercise of this gift.

Many people do not live in this kind of environment, however, and so they need to look to the Lord for direction to find those people who can be their prayer support, encouragement, and accountability team outside of their immediate family. Perhaps you are single, married to an unbeliever, or are living with unsaved family members. Find prayer warriors to meet with and be encouraged in your walk with the Lord through them. This requires communicating with them on a regular basis and meeting with them individually or in a group. A weekly Bible study group through your church home fellowship ministry is a good place to start.

Principles of Accountability

Whatever your situation, you need to place yourself under the authority of church leadership. There are two important principles related to this that you need to keep in mind. The first principle is to always have a third party with you if you are meeting with a pastor or church leadership team member of the opposite sex. Twice in my life, I have experienced the church-wide devastation of pastors falling because of sexual sin with church members who found themselves frequently thrown together under the guise of ministry. I remember reading a story a long time ago about Billy Graham's concern that even his reputation be unsullied in this way. He refused to be interviewed by a female journalist at his home, even with other people present. Instead, he met her for the interview in a very public restaurant with several of his colleagues present.

The second principle is that, no matter what your family dynamics involve regarding saved and unsaved members, scriptural directives need to be followed. The Bible clearly states our roles as family members. Whether your family understands and supports your gift or not, the biblical norm for families is outlined in Colossians 3:18–21: "Wives, submit yourselves unto your own husbands, as it is fit in the Lord. Husbands, love your wives, and be not bitter against them. Children, obey your parents in all things: for this is well pleasing unto the Lord. Fathers, provoke not your children to anger, lest they be discouraged."

Ephesians 5:21–32 (ESV) makes it clear that the relationship between husband and wife is to represent the relationship between Christ and His Church to the world around us:

> ... submitting to one another out of reverence for Christ. Wives, submit to your own husbands, as to the Lord. For the husband is

the head of the wife even as Christ is the head of the church, His body, and is Himself its Savior. Now as the church submits to Christ, so also wives should submit in everything to their husbands. Husbands, love your wives, as Christ loved the church and gave Himself up for her, that He might sanctify her, having cleansed her by the washing of water with the word, so that He might present the church to Himself in splendor, without spot or wrinkle or any such thing, that she might be holy and without blemish. In the same way husbands should love their wives as their own bodies. He who loves his wife loves himself. For no one ever hated his own flesh, but nourishes and cherishes it, just as Christ does the church, because we are members of His body. "Therefore a man shall leave his father and mother and hold fast to his wife, and the two shall become one flesh." This mystery is profound, and I am saying that it refers to Christ and the church.

While God has stated His will regarding avoidance of being unequally yoked with unbelievers (2 Corinthians 6:14), there are those Christians who are married to unbelievers. This could be because of a decision to marry made outside of God's will or as a result of one of the spouses accepting Christ as Lord and Savior without the other following suit. As to those married to unbelievers, the Bible also has clear directions for the believer in the relationship. It has to do with the Christian imperative to preach the gospel to the world, starting at home (Acts 1:8). First Corinthians 7:12–16 specifically tells us:

> If any brother has a wife that believes not, and she be pleased to dwell with him, let him not put her away. And the woman which has a husband that believeth not, and if he be pleased to dwell with her, let her not leave him. For the unbelieving husband is sanctified by the wife, and the unbelieving wife is sanctified by the husband: else were your children unclean; but now are they holy. But if the unbelieving departs, let him depart. A brother or a sister is not under bondage in such cases: but God has called us to peace. For what know you, O wife, whether you shall save your husband? Or how know you, O man, whether you shall save your wife?

Scriptural directives also call us to submission to the spiritual leaders, our pastors, whom God has placed over us. Hebrews 13:17 says, "Obey them that have the rule over you, and submit yourselves: for they watch for your souls, as they that must give account, that they may do it with joy, and not with grief: for that is unprofitable for you."

While we may recognize our giftedness as a spiritual discerner, we will have to rely on the Holy Spirit to direct our families to do so. The very bizarreness of our experiences is unnerving to those who have never experienced it themselves. "Trish" (not her real name) shared that she simply doesn't disclose her feelings and perceptions to anyone except to those who she knows understand this gift. For instance, her first understanding of the ill feelings she had in certain situations as the manifestation of discerning of spirits came as a result of hearing Dr. Stieglitz speak on the subject of spiritual warfare. She approached him afterward to ask about her experiences with the perception of evil, and he helped her understand that she was experiencing the gift of discerning of spirits.

Summary

Because of the intrusive nature of our gift into the spiritual world and the danger we pose to our enemy as a result, we need to make sure we have a solid prayer and accountability team. For me, the primary person who has taken on that role is my husband.

However, for whatever reason, not everyone with the gift of discerning of spirits has a home in which they are able to find their key support. Those people need to seek prayer support and accountability elsewhere. A good place to prayerfully start is in a small home Bible study group. Attention needs to be paid to the principles of accountability in the discerning of spirits. Be sure you never meet alone with a member of the opposite sex and always follow scriptural precepts in your relationships.

A Few Final Thoughts

Discerning of spirits is one of the many gifts that the Holy Spirit gives to whom He wants and at the levels that He decides. No one gift is more valuable than any other. Each gift needs to be developed and used at the appropriate times and places according to God's direction.

The focus of this book has been the gift of discerning of spirits because it is so frequently misunderstood and has so often been neglected as a result. This gift of discerning of spirits is God's radar for spiritual warfare. Besides the preview of coming attacks on both the Church and individuals, outcomes also include ministry to people through prayer, godly counsel, exhortation, and/or a recognition of the need for help (i.e., righteous action or spiritual warfare). Since Satan currently holds this world hostage to sin, Christians gifted with discerning of spirits are necessary for the protection of the Church and other Christians.

Every Christian is given gifts of the Holy Spirit and the calling to use them for God's glory at the point of salvation. In order to carry out what we are called and gifted to do, each Christian must maintain a pure relationship with our Lord and Savior, Jesus Christ, unhindered by unconfessed sin. We do this by making sure we have in place the "weapons of resistance" provided by God—Truth, Righteousness, the Gospel of Peace, Salvation, Faith, the Word of God, Prayer, and Alertness. As we mature in our understanding of God's character through meditation on the Word of God, He reveals to us what His will is regarding our gifts and calling.

In the case of discerning of spirits, this process includes prayer, looking for patterns, recognition of physical anomalies and emotional impacts that events, people, and places have on us, and the God-given, God-directed, and God-glorifying outcomes of these events.

In the face of current world events and the evil behind them, it is easy to be discouraged. However, God said that this would happen (1 Timothy 4:1). We are clearly in the latter days when people will pay attention to the doctrines of demons. God is calling and equipping more and more people to be the gatekeepers. Having a continual awareness of the spiritual realm, those of us called and gifted in discerning of spirits are able to act as an advanced warning system to protect His Church and His people.

Jesus Christ won the victory on the cross once and for all. From Him, we have the power, by faith, to refute that which would suggest otherwise. God also gives us all that we need in order to do what He calls us to do. As we exercise and mature in the gift the Holy Spirit gave us at the point of salvation, we need to remember this:

"Greater is He that is in you, than he that is in the world."

(1 John 4:4b)

Additional Reading Suggestions

Angels

Angels: Elect and Evil by C. Fred Dickason

Angels: Fantasy, Mystery, or Reality? by John Williams

Men and Angels by R. E. Harlow

The Holy Spirit

The Person and Work of the Holy Spirit by Samuel Ridout

The Holy Spirit: Lord and Life-Giver by John Williams

Gifts of the Holy Spirit

The Baptism and Gifts of the Holy Spirit
by Merrill Unger

Gifts of the Spirit by Ronald E. Baxter

Spiritual Warfare

The Handbook for Spiritual Warfare
by Edward F. Murphy

Spiritual Warfare in the Believer's Life by Charles
Spurgeon (Robert Hall, ed.)

*Spiritual Warfare: Victory over the Powers of This Dark
World* by Timothy W. Warner

*Breaking Satanic Bondage: Intensive Training in Spiritual
Warfare* by Gil Stieglitz

Prayer

George Mueller of Bristol: His Life of Prayer and Faith
by Arthur T. Pierson

How to Pray by R. A. Torrey

The Believer's School of Prayer by Andrew Murray

Does It Pay to Pray? by Carl T. Knott and
William MacDonald

Rees Howell, Intercessor by Norman Grubb

Personal Christian Growth

Knowing God by J. I. Packer

Spiritual Disciplines of a C.H.R.I.S.T.I.A.N. by Gil Stieglitz

Delighting in God: A Key to Effective Spiritual Leadership by Gil Stieglitz

The Cost of Discipleship by Dietrich Bonhoeffer

The Practice of the Presence of God by Brother Lawrence

Overcoming Temptation and Sin

The Bondage Breaker by Neil Anderson

Victory over the Darkness by Neil Anderson

Reclaiming Surrendered Ground: Protecting Your Family from Spiritual Attacks by Jim Logan

Satan and Demons

Satan: His Person, Work, Place, and Destiny by F. C. Jennings

The Adversary: The Christian versus Demonic Activity by Mark Bubeck

The Powers of Darkness by Clinton Arnold

The Satan of Scripture by W. A. Mason

Demonology by Merrill Unger

Demon Possession and the Christian: A New Perspective
by C. Fred Dickason

Power Encounters

Power Encounters Among Christians in the Western World by Kevin Springer

Weapons of Spiritual Warfare

Secrets of God's Armor: Building Strong Christians for the Battle by Gil Stieglitz

Marriage/Relationships

Loving Your Marriage Enough to Protect It by Jerry B. Jenkins

Marital Intelligence by Gil Stieglitz

God's Radical Plan for Wives by Gil and Dana Stieglitz with Jennifer Edwards

Becoming a Godly Husband by Gil Stieglitz

Narratives of Miraculous Contemporary Discerning of Spirits

A Present Help: Standing on the Promises of God by Marie Monson

Life Miracles by Kevin Dyer

Rethinking Discernment: The Argument for Chiastic Order in 1 Corinthians 12:10

In order to understand the biblical basis of discerning of spirits in spiritual warfare beyond the recognition of false teachers and prophets, we need to look deeply into 1 Corinthians 12:10. In this verse, the term "discerning of spirits" occurs as part of a list of gifts given by the Holy Spirit (vv. 4–11):

> Now there are diversities of gifts, but the same Spirit. And there are differences of administrations, but the same Lord. And there are diversities of operations, but it is the same God which works all in all. But the manifestation of the Spirit is given to every man to profit withal. For to one is given by the spirit the word of wisdom; to another the word of knowledge by the same Spirit; To another faith by the same Spirit; to another the gifts

of healing by the same Spirit; To another the working of miracles; to another prophecy; to another discerning of spirits; to another diverse kinds of tongues; to another the interpretation of tongues: But all these works that one and the selfsame Spirit, dividing to every man severally as he will.

In this passage, the Holy Spirit achieves a unity of purpose and momentum through a diversity of gifts. At first reading, the writer of these verses seems to have made an intentional sequence of the gifts, relating them in such a way that each appears to lead to the other in binary associations—the word of wisdom leads to the word of knowledge; neither healings nor miracles can be done without faith; prophecy given requires discerning of spirits; and tongues require the interpretation thereof.

Upon closer examination and literarily speaking, however, the binary form occurs twice (vv. 8, 9) followed by a quinary[1] in verse 10. Granted, this designation of verses was the choice of the translators for the original King James Bible and not a part of the original Greek New Testament. Nevertheless, the form of these verses makes it clear why those translators chose the verse divisions.

---

[1] The term "quinary" refers to an arrangement of five items.

While the two binaries have an AB form to them, the quinary has a chiastic[2] pattern (ABCBA form). Verse 10 starts with the working of miracles (a gift of service) and then cites prophecy (a gift of speech).[3] At the end of the verse, the diverse kinds of tongues (a gift of speech) is followed by the interpretation of the tongues (a gift of service). Standing alone, discerning of spirits is the centerpiece and focus of this verse, which seems to indicate a shared usage on both sides of the pattern. According to the implication of the form of this verse, discerning of spirits is not only directed at preaching and teaching but also at service according to the distribution of the gifts by the Spirit of God. It also indicates that this gift is a particular gift not granted to every Christian, as would be indicated by discernment through maturity described above.

---

[2] Chiastic pattern (also known as palistrophes, chiasms, symmetric structures, ring structures, and concentric structures) is a frequently used literary structure that places concepts or ideas in a symmetrical order for emphasis on the inmost concept (C). This stress on the centerpiece shows that the other ideas all lead up to the middle idea or concept. Evidently a mnemonic device for memorization with a view to oral transmission, this structure was also used most notably in the *Torah, Beowulf,* and *Paradise Lost.*

[3] From Liberty University, *The King James Study Bible* (Rio de Janeiro: Thomas Nelson, 1988), 1781. *The King James Study Bible* includes a footnote for this function indicating that the gift of prophecy is no longer needed today now that the canon of Scripture is complete. According to this reference, preaching is the expression of this gift in today's Church. LaSor, Hubbard, and Bush, on the other hand, define a prophet as a person who acts as the voice and interpreter of a god. Given that God's redeeming purpose culminates in Jesus Christ, all prophecy must somehow point to Him. Prophecy is, then, fulfilled in Christ, a definition supported by biblical evidence (Ibid, p. 230), which would give this gift a viable role even for today (Romans 12:6). William Sanford LaSor, David Allan Hubbard, Frederic William Bush, *Old Testament Survey* (Grand Rapids: William B. Eerdmans, 1996), 122.

BIBLIOGRAPHY

Anderson, Neil T. *The Bondage Breaker.* Eugene: Harvest House, 1993.

—. *Victory Over the Darkness.* Ventura, CA: Regal Books, 2000.

Arnold, Clinton. *The Powers of Darkness.* Downers Grove, IL: InterVarsity, 1992.

Billheimer, Paul E. *Destined for the Throne.* Fort Washington, PA: Christian Literature Crusade, 1975.

Bonhoeffer, Dietrich. *The Cost of Discipleship.* London: Macmillan, 1961.

Bubeck, Mark I. *The Adversary: The Christian Versus Demonic Activity.* Chicago: Moody Bible Institute, 1975.

Dickason, C. Fred. *Demon Possession and the Christian: A New Perspective.* Chicago, IL: Moody Press, 1987

Dyer, Kevin G. *Life Miracles.* Hoffman Estates, IL: Bright Hope International, 2010.

Foxe, John and W. Grinton Berry, ed. *Foxe's Book of Martyrs.* Grand Rapids: Fleming H. Revell, 2004.

Jeffcoat, John L. ed. and Dr. Craig H. Lampe. *English Bible History Article and Timeline.* 2012. http://www.greatsite.com/timeline-english-bible-history/.

Jennings, F. C. *Satan: His Person, Work, Place, and Destiny.* New York: Loiseaux Brothers, 1910.

Kellogg, Howard W. *Life in the Blood: A Study of Atonement Upon Altar and Cross.* New York: Charles C. Cook, n.d.

Knott, Carl T. Jr. and William MacDonald. *Does It Pay to Pray?* Scarborough, Ontario, Canada: Everyday Publishers, Inc., 1994.

Kuehn, Pastor Gregory. "Terrorist Intel, Part 2." Sierra Bible Church, September 26, 2010. Reno, Nevada, n.d.

LaSor, William Sanford, David Allan Hubbard, Frederic William Bush. *Old Testament Survey.* Grand Rapids: William B. Eerdmans, 1996.

Lewis, C. S. *The Best of C. S. Lewis.* Grand Rapids, MI: Baker Book House, 1977.

—. *The Last Battle.* New York: Macmillan Publishing Company, 1970.

Liberty University. *The King James Study Bible.* Rio de Janeiro: Thomas Nelson, 1988.

Logan, Jim. *Reclaiming Surrendered Ground: Protecting Your Family from Spiritual Attacks.* Chicago: Moody Publishers, 1995.

MacArthur, John. "Discernment: Spiritual Survival for a Church in Crisis." Grace to You. http://www.gty.org/resources/positions/P02/discernment-spiritual-survival-for-a-church-incrisis, n.d. [accessed March 21, 2013].

MacDonald, William. *Believers Bible Commentary New Testament.* Wichita, KS: A & O Press, 1989.

—. *Believer's Bible Commentary Old Testament.* Nashville: Thomas Nelson Publishers, 1992.

Mason, W. A. *The Satan of Scripture.* Toronto: A. Sims, 1901.

Matrisciana, Caryl. *Out of India.* Menifee, CA: Caryl Productions, 2008.

—. "Wide Is The Gate: The Emerging New Christianity, Volume I." Menifee, CA, 2011. DVD.

Monson, Marie. *A Present Help: Standing on the Promises of God.* Santa Anna: Calvary Chapel Publishing, 2008.

Morris, William, Ed. *The American Heritage Dictionary of the English Language.* New York: American Heritage Publishing Co., Inc. and Houghton Mifflin Company, 1971.

Murphy, Edward F. *The Handbook for Spiritual Warfare.* Nashville: Thomas Nelson, Inc., 2003.

Murray, Andrew. *The Believer's School of Prayer.* Minneapolis, MN: Bethany House Publishers, 1982.

Murray, John. "Fall, The" in Merrill C. Tenney, ed., *Zondervan Encyclopedia of the Bible.* Grand Rapids: Zondervan, 1977.

Ogilvie, Lloyd John. *God's Best for My Life.* Eugene, OR: Harvest House Publishing, 1981.

Ovitt, Ronald. "Do You Have the Spiritual Gift of Discernment?" (accessed 3/13/2011) http://spiritualgifts.wordpress.com/2007/04/14/do-you-have-the-spiritual-gift-of-discernment/. April 14, 2007.

Packer, J. I. *Knowing God.* Downers Grove: InterVarsity Press, 1973.

Peretti, Frank. *This Present Darkness.* Wheaton, IL: Crossway Books, 1992.

Pierson, Arthur T. *George Muller of Bristol: His Life of Prayer and Faith.* Grand Rapids, MI: Kregel Publications, 1999.

Ridout, Samuel. *The Person and Work of the Holy Spirit.* New York: Loiseaux Brothers, n.d.

Sheets, Dutch. *Intercessory Prayer—How God Can Use Your Prayers to Move Heaven and Earth.* Ventura, CA: Regal from Gospel Light, 1996.

Springer, Kevin. *Power Encounters Among Christians in the Western World.* San Francisco: Harper and Row, 1988.

Spurgeon, Charles and Robert Hall, ed. *Spiritual Warfare in a Believer's Life.* Lynnwood, WA: Emerald Books, 1993.

Stedman, Ray C. *Spiritual Warfare.* Waco, TX: Word Books, 1971.

Stieglitz, Gil. *Breaking Satanic Bondage: Intensive Training in Spiritual Warfare.* Roseville, CA: Principles To Live By, 2009.

—. *Spiritual Disciplines of a C.H.R.I.S.T.I.A.N.: Intensive Training in Christian Spirituality.* Minden, NV: Thriving Churches Int'l, Inc., 2011.

Strong, James. *Strong's Exhaustive Concordance of the Bible Together with Dictionaries of the Hebrew and Greek Words of the Original.* MacDonald Publishing Company, n.d.

Tenney, M. C. *Galatians, The Charter of Christian Liberty.* Grand Rapids: Eerdmans, 1950.

The Holy Bible: Authorized (King James) Version. London: Eyre and Spottiswoode Ltd., 1968. Cambridge University Press is the Crown's patentee in the UK.

The Holy Bible, English Standard Version. Wheaton: Crossway, a publishing ministry of Good News Publishers, 2001

Torrey, R. A. *How to Pray.* New Kensington, PA: Whitaker House, 1984.

Unger, Merrill F. *The Baptism & Gifts of the Holy Spirit.* Chicago: Moody Press, 1974.

Vine, W. E. *An Expository Dictionary of New Testament Words.* Lynchburg, VA: Old Time Gospel Hour, 1952.

Warner, Timothy W. *Spiritual Warfare: Victory over the Powers of This Dark World.* Wheaton, IL: Crossway, 1991.

Williams, John. *The Holy Spirit, Lord and Life-Giver.* Neptune: Loiseaux Brothers, 1980.

Wimber, John and Kevin Springer. *Power Healing.* San Francisco: Harper Collins Publishers, 1987.

Dr. Susan Merritt is a prayer warrior who has helped church congregations recognize the true source of spiritual warfare and the lies behind hindered ministries, broken lives, and divided relationships.

Susan taught in Northern California elementary schools for more than twenty years. Once she and her husband retired, they moved to Northern Nevada to be closer to family. They have three adult children who are each married and have children of their own.

Dr. Merritt holds a Ph.D. in Biblical Studies with a focus on Spiritual Warfare from Newburgh Theological Seminary. She is also the author of *The Culture of Hope Founded on Faith* and *Reformation Trilogy.* Her new book, *Faith 2.0: Finding Hope When the Bottom Falls Out,* is scheduled for publication in 2025. To contact Dr. Merritt, go to susanmerrittphd.com.

www.ingramcontent.com/pod-product-compliance
Lightning Source LLC
Chambersburg PA
CBHW021223090426
42740CB00006B/357